LON

THE PARDONER'S PROLOGUE AND TALE

Geoffrey Chaucer

Editors:
Linda Cookson
Bryan Loughrey

Editors: Linda Cookson and Bryan Loughrey

Titles in the series:

CONTENTS

PREFACE

Like all professional groups, literary critics have developed their own specialised language. This is not necessarily a bad thing. Sometimes complex concepts can only be described in a terminology far removed from everyday speech. Academic jargon, however, creates an unnecessary barrier between the critic and the intelligent but less practised reader.

This danger is particularly acute where scholarly books and articles are re-packaged for a student audience. Critical anthologies, for example, often contain extracts from longer studies originally written for specialists. Deprived of their original context, these passages can puzzle and at times mislead. The essays in this volume, however, are all specially commissioned, self-contained works, written with the needs of students firmly in mind.

This is not to say that the contributors — all experienced critics and teachers — have in any way attempted to simplify the complexity of the issues with which they deal. On the contrary, they explore the central problems of the text from a variety of critical perspectives, reaching conclusions which are challenging and at times mutually contradictory.

They try, however, to present their arguments in direct, accessible language and to work within the limitations of scope and length which students inevitably face. For this reason, essays are generally rather briefer than is the practice; they address quite specific topics; and, in line with examination requirements, they incorporate precise textual detail into the body of the discussion.

They offer, therefore, working examples of the kind of essay-writing skills which students themselves are expected to develop. Their diversity, however, should act as a reminder that in the field of literary studies there is no such thing as a 'model' answer. Good essays are the outcome of a creative engagement with literature, of sensitive, attentive reading and careful thought. We hope that those contained in this volume will encourage students to return to the most important starting point of all, the text itself, with renewed excitement and the determination to explore more fully their own critical responses.

How to use this volume

Obviously enough, you should start by reading the text in question. The one assumption that all the contributors make is that you are already familiar with this. It would be helpful, of course, to have read further — perhaps other works by the same author or by influential contemporaries. But we don't assume that you have yet had the opportunity to do this and any references to historical background or to other works of literature are explained.

You should, perhaps, have a few things to hand. It is always a good idea to keep a copy of the text nearby when reading critical studies. You will almost certainly want to consult it when checking the context of quotations or pausing to consider the validity of the critic's interpretation. You should also try to have access to a good dictionary, and ideally a copy of a dictionary of literary terms as well. The contributors have tried to avoid jargon and to express themselves clearly and directly. But inevitably there will be occasional words or phrases with which you are unfamiliar. Finally, we would encourage you to make notes, summarising not just the argument of each essay but also your own responses to what you have read. So keep a pencil and notebook at the ready.

Suitably equipped, the best thing to do is simply begin with whichever topic most interests you. We have deliberately organised each volume so that the essays may be read in any order. One consequence of this is that, for the sake of clarity and self-containment, there is occasionally a degree of overlap between essays. But at least you are not forced to follow one — fairly arbitrary — reading sequence.

Each essay is followed by brief 'Afterthoughts', designed to highlight points of critical interest. But remember, these are only there to remind you that it is *your* responsibility to question what you read. The essays printed here are not a series of 'model' answers to be slavishly imitated and in no way should they be regarded as anything other than a guide or stimulus for your own thinking. We hope for a critically involved response: 'That was interesting. But if *I* were tackling the topic . . .!'

Read the essays in this spirit and you'll pick up many of the skills of critical composition in the process. We have, however, tried to provide more explicit advice in 'A practical guide to essay writing'. You may find this helpful, but do not imagine it offers any magic formulas. The quality of your essays ultimately depends on the quality of your engagement with literary texts. We hope this volume spurs you on to read these with greater understanding and to explore your responses in greater depth.

A note on the text

Unless otherwise stated, all references are to Fragment VI of *The Riverside Chaucer*, Third Edition, edited by Larry D Benson (Oxford, 1988). In that edition the *Introduction to the Pardoner's Tale* begins at line 287, *The Pardoner's Prologue* begins at line 329, and *The Pardoner's Tale* begins at line 463. Anyone working from an edition of *The Pardoner's Prologue and Tale* which begins at line 1 will have to make the necessary subtraction (of approximately 286 lines, but editions vary considerably in respect to line numbering).

Cedric Watts

Cedric Watts is Professor of English at Sussex University, and author of many scholarly publications.

ESSAY

Problem-areas of *The Pardoner's Tale*

In my view, the main problem-areas of *The Pardoner's Tale* include these. First, the relationship between the tale, its prologue and the depiction of the Pardoner in the *General Prologue*. Second, the significance of the old man who is so crucial to the story. Third, the extent of the ironies. I discuss these matters in that order.

1

The Pardoner has remarkably problematic genitalia: his testicles seem to vanish and return. In the *General Prologue*, he is vividly depicted as weird, freakish, effeminate and emasculate; yet, in *The Pardoner's Prologue* and *The Pardoner's Tale*, he seems rapidly to grow in power, potency and stature. Initially, he is seen as the contemptible paramour of the revolting Summoner: he sings 'Com hider, love, to me!', and the Summoner 'bar to hym a stif burdoun' (suggestive phrasing, meaning 'provided him with a strong bass accompaniment' but hinting at 'gave him a stiff underpinning' — a homosexual innuendo). His yellow hair hangs down over his shoulders; his voice is as small as a goat's; and, if the reference to a goat suggests virility, this suggestion is promptly erased by the following lines, which say:

> No berd hadde he, ne nevere sholde have;
> As smothe it was as it were late shave.
> I trowe he were a gelding or a mare.

(I, ll.689–691)

A gelding is a castrated horse, while a mare is, obviously, a female; and commentators usually make sense of that last line by declaring the Pardoner 'a eunuch or a homosexual'. What is stressed is that the Pardoner lacks testicles; what is implied is that he is the effeminate partner in a homosexual pairing. (R P Miller once suggested that he represents the sinner known to theologians as the 'spiritual eunuch', 'who, sterile in good works, does not have the organs of spiritual generation and fertility.'[1]) Yet, in his preamble, the Pardoner declares:

> Nay, I wol drynke licour of the vyne
> And have a joly wenche in every toun.

(ll.452–453)[2]

This doesn't fit, and cannot be made to fit. That he likes wine is no problem; but that 'a gelding or a mare' should be heterosexually promiscuous is anomalous. Some parts of this characterisation (the hypocrisy, the corrupt vending of 'holy relics', and his rhetorical skills which enable him to exploit the gullible) remain constant; but sexually he is impossibly inconsistent. At the end of his tale, he invites the Host to pay to kiss the fraudulent relics, and the Host declares:

> I wolde I hadde thy coillons in myn hond
> In stide of relikes or of seintuarie.
> Lat kutte hem of, I wol thee helpe hem carie;
> They shul be shryned in an hogges toord!

(ll.952–955)

---

[1] Robert P Miller, 'Chaucer's Pardoner and the Scriptural Eunuch', in *Chaucer Criticism: The Canterbury Tales*, ed. R J Schoeck and J Taylor (Notre Dame, Indiana, 1960), p. 226.
[2] See 'A note on the text' (p. 8) regarding line references.

This splendid invective makes sense only if the Pardoner is imagined as having cullions (testicles) that could conceivably be cut off. What seems to have happened is this: Chaucer, in developing the Pardoner's character, has changed it, so that the freakish eunuch of the *General Prologue* — sexually impotent — has become, in various ways, a formidably potent figure. He is potent not merely in the trivial sense of being a successful lecher who has 'a joly wenche in every toun' but in a subtler sense: his oratory is disturbingly powerful; for all his avowed hypocrisy, his tale has provided a fierce *memento mori* and warning against avarice and dissolute living.

Of course, it can then be argued that the Pardoner is implausibly inconsistent, in that he expects his auditors to pay for his intercession even though he has previously revealed to them his gross hypocrisy and charlatanism. His preamble offers a gleefully frank account of the devices by which he tricks his victims; his tale, as he forewarns the hearers, conforms to his strategy of excoriating avarice (so as to make his victims the more ready to pay for his aid); and yet, at its termination, he nevertheless urges the fellow-pilgrims to get their money out. If he's the cunning trickster that he claims to be, is it really plausible that he would spoil his own sales-pitch by so candid an initial revelation of his turpitude?

One theory is that his inconsistency is the result of drunkenness; and certainly the Pardoner, who likes a draught 'of moyste and corny ale', has paused for such refreshment before beginning his prologue. On the other hand, his autobiographical revelations and his subsequent presentation of a sermon are delivered with a lucidity and adroitness which indicate no befuddled wits. A more plausible theory is that, having recounted the extent of his turpitude, the Pardoner tells a tale so forcefully effective that his hearers are deeply impressed; and, on seeing that they are so spellbound, he gambles that they may after all be fooled by his customary sales-talk; but the Host, annoyed by having been singled out as especially sinful and in need of intercession, then coarsely breaks the spell and provokes general laughter at the Pardoner's expense. A third (and rather more convincing) explanation is that the Pardoner is partly an impressively realistic characterisation and partly an imaginative pretext to enable Chaucer to develop an interesting range of ironic, comic and rhetorical possibilities. Chaucer enjoyed creating the Pardoner's self-revelations; he enjoyed the deployment of his story; and he enjoyed leading the Pardoner to a point of over-confidence at which he could hilariously be dumbfounded by the Host. So there occurs some friction between Pardoner as consistent character and Pardoner as occasion of lively literary effects. The consequent inconsistency is largely justified by the entertaining results.

This is not to gainsay the local persuasiveness and astonishing tonal mastery of much of this sequence. Perhaps the finest moment comes when the Pardoner says:

> And lo, sires, thus I preche.
> And Jhesu Crist, that is oure soules leche,
> So graunte yow his pardoun to receyve,
> For that is beste; I wol yow nat deceyve.
> But, sires, o word forgat I in my tale:
> I have relikes and pardoun in my male

(ll.915–920)

It is as though, for a few moments, a sincere and pious self emerges from the Pardoner's corruption; and that self invokes the *true* pardoner, Jesus Christ. 'I wol yow nat deceyve' seems to be delivered in quiet, honest tones. Then, after a pause, the fallen figure resumes the voice of corruption (with 'But, sires, o word forgat I in my tale'); and the old but perennial game of the confidence-trickster recommences.

2

In his tale, the three young sinners who hope to kill Death encounter a strange old man. That old man is clearly a symbolic figure, but what he symbolises has long been a matter of critical dispute. One suggestion is that he is the Wandering Jew, the accursed figure who, for his sins, is doomed to wander the earth endlessly; another is that he is Death personified; another is that he is a messenger of death; another is that he is the devil; and yet another is that he is *vetus homo*, i.e., fallen or corrupt man (as opposed to the 'new man', humanity redeemed by

Christel).[3] Single specific identifications may make us overlook the fact that if we recognise a literary entity as symbolic it is precisely because that entity clearly bears a *mysterious* burden of significance. William Blake's 'sick rose'[4] is no ordinary rose and may represent corrupted sexuality, or love oppressed by religious restraints, or a particular woman who has become corrupted, or even England itself; we recognise the rose as symbolic because it is richly suggestive and is likely to suggest different meanings to different readers, and we are not given an authorial decipherment which would resolve the ambiguity by narrowing the options to one. What differentiates the symbolic from the allegoric is that whereas the allegoric has a clear and single burden of significance, the symbolic always includes an area of doubt, of the unresolved.

The old man in the tale is, to some extent, a realistic figure; a thin, aged person, weary and melancholy, who warns the young swaggerers to respect the elderly and who repeatedly offers the pious hope that God may be with them and may save them. What is not realistic is that he seems to be doomed to an incredibly protracted old age: Mother Earth will not open to receive him; Death declines to take him; no young person will change places with him; and he must wander 'As longe tyme as it is Goddes wille'. This links him to accursed undying wanderers of folk-lore and legend; yet there is nothing in the old man's narrative to suggest that he has committed some sin for which the wanderings are a punishment. He seems uncanny, eldritch, yet still poignant and pathetic. Nevertheless, when the young questers seek guidance, he is prompt to tell them (in the event, accurately) where death can be found:

> . . . turne up this croked wey,
> For in that grove I lafte hym . . .

(ll.761–762)

And this gives him a more sinister quality; for, though he cannot die himself, he knows death's location, and his advice

---

[3] Miller, pp. 226–227.
[4] Blake, 'The Sick Rose', in *Poetry and Prose of William Blake*, ed. G Keynes (London, 1956), p. 71.

will lead the men to the hoard of gold and to their mutual destruction. He's a fusion of different elements, then: a piously reproachful old man; a constant wanderer denied the peace of death; an agent of destruction; a reminder of God's mercy but also of God's stern justice for sinners; and a riddling seer, prophet or mage: a figure of folk-lore related to aged Tiresias, the blind Theban prophet, or to the Cumaean Sybil who spoke in riddles and bewailed her immortality of perpetual senility. When he cries, 'Leeve mooder, leet me in!' (1.731), begging to be buried at last in the ground, it's a cry that many a lonely arthritic pensioner today could understand; but it also gives the uncanny suggestion that he's the weary child of Mother Earth herself rather than of any normal parents. His power as a literary creation derives from the combination of question-begging particulars and an answer-frustrating inner opacity; he embodies many possibilities, many implications; and the trickiest task for a critic may be to preserve that sense of the rich potential of significance without narrowing it to one final dominant meaning.

3

The sequence of narratives in which that old man can be seen as a focal centre contains irony within irony within irony. The three roisterers sought to kill death and were killed by him; they thought they had found treasure instead of death, but the treasure was death's bait; through avarice and arrogance they destroyed each other; each biter was bit. An outer circle of irony, as the Pardoner explains, is that a sermon whose most memorable passage warns against avarice is designed to gratify the Pardoner's avarice by frightening the hearers into generosity. Some of the ironies bounce to and fro: the Pardoner denounces the roisterers who drink and blaspheme, but he himself drinks and blasphemes; the more he illustrates their foolhardy neglect of divine wrath, the more he seems in danger of incurring it himself. If the tale tells of the biters who are bitten, the teller is bitten in turn: his 'nemesis' is his humiliation when the Host denounces his fraudulence. This list of ironies can be elaborated in immense detail, given the relish with which the Pardoner cites text after text to denounce sins of which he is a conspicuous partaker. Perhaps the major irony which coordinates all the others is that inherent in the Christian view of humanity: that we are all fallen beings, sinful and worthy of damnation; but we, if Christians, also have divine guidance and access to the possibility of divine grace and mercy. Hence, each man is *homo duplex*, a double man contaminated with the sins of Adam yet enlightened by the word of Christ. As Sir Philip Sidney remarked, 'Our erected wit maketh us to know what perfection is, and yet our infected will keepeth us from reaching unto it.'[5] In the Pardoner, in most extreme form, Chaucer depicts both man's 'erected wit' and 'infected will'.

If such moral analysis seems to make the sequence too solemn, we then sense a still larger irony. Even the moral and religious issues which are so sharply focused in the sequence are put into a larger perspective. There is a quality of creative verve and virtuosity which implies Chaucer's aesthetic delight in the imaginative vistas he is creating; the moralist operates within the arena of keenly engaged creativity. And this, surely, is why the ending seems so appropriate. When the Pardoner is speechless with rage and the Host seems scornfully triumphant, at that point the Knight steps in to reconcile with remarkable courtesy and impartiality the two antagonists. He invites 'sire Pardoner' and 'sire Hoost' to kiss and be reconciled: 'And, as we diden, lat us laughe and pleye'. The three roisterers had become divided against each other and had perished; the corrupt Pardoner and the vulgar Host, after fierce division, are reconciled by the courteous magnanimity of the Knight: harmony and good humour are restored. In such moments, the genial tolerance of Chaucer, writing in the fourteenth century, seems to set standards of civilisation which the modern world, so often riven by grim and relentless ideological disputes, has yet to appreciate and actualise.

When the Knight step in as peace-maker and harmony is restored to the band of travellers, the previous theological wrangles about sin and the roads to salvation and damnation

---

[5] Sidney, 'An Apology for Poetry', in *English Critical Essays*, ed. Edmund D Jones (London, 1922, reprinted 1965), p. 8.

seem, for a while, to dwindle and diminish; indeed, to a modern reader, they may look like a form of ideological lunacy: part of a system of superstition and mystification maintained by church and state as a mode of social control. The modern response may not be wholly anachronistic, for Chaucer often enough mocks theological niceties and commends good-humoured sociability. Nevertheless, the man with the power to impose reconciliation on the Pardoner and the Host is, predictably, the Knight: a noble and socially powerful figure. His authority as peace-maker in England derives in part from his reputation as warlord abroad — the *General Prologue* had specified his long career as a campaigner who fights and, in the name of Christ, slaughters the so-called infidels.

Many of Chaucer's ironies are intentional, having been adroitly and astutely deployed. Others may well be unintentional, a consequence of the fact that he is registering without resolving the ideological confusions and contradictions of his period. Sometimes *moral* intentionality, which seeks to commend good moral examples, conflicts with *imaginative* intentionality, which seeks to create vivid, credible and fascinating characters. The poor Parson sets a virtuous moral example, but in the *General Prologue* he seems merely an idealised stereotype; it's the sinful Pardoner who comes vividly to life and stamps himself on the memory. When we have listed all the Pardoner's sins and failings, and when we have estimated the vast extent of his hypocrisy, we should nevertheless notice that he provides more interesting and engaging company for us than do the more virtuous figures. In that respect, the ultimate irony of this sequence of *The Canterbury Tales* may be that the Pardoner has, after all, won his audience over, though it is an audience larger than the original band of pilgrims; it is an audience of millions of readers which extends through time from the fourteenth century to the present day and beyond.

AFTERTHOUGHTS

1

How important is it for a fictional character to be consistent?

2

What distinction does Watts draw between symbol and allegory (page 13)?

3

Explain the relevance to Watts's argument of the concept of *homo duplex* (page 15).

4

How can we *know* which of Chaucer's ironies are 'intentional' (page 16)?

Richard Smith

Richard Smith is Head of English at The Lakes School, Windermere and an experienced teacher of A level.

ESSAY

The Pardoner's Prologue and Tale —
poetry for performance

I've had problems with Chaucer — as a reader, in 'studying' him, and as a teacher. The first hurdle, too often forgotten by academic critics and teachers who have successfully vaulted it and apparently with gusto, was of course the language. Having shambled around that one by regular and tedious shuffling of the pages of glossaries, I came up against a sense of his apparent naïvety and simplicity when compared to the more modern literature which I was more interested in when I first started to read him. Then, in reading a tale like the Pardoner's, I not only felt for myself the apparent inconsistencies in the psychology of the character and his actions, but found the critics and teachers, to whom I looked for help, agonising over it also and coming up with explanations that often looked unconvincing or more like excuses.

The turning point for me was when I put some time into learning to read Chaucer aloud reasonably fluently. Some of the people who introduced me to Chaucer had advised me to do this, of course, but I didn't. I wish I had done it earlier. Only when I came to do so did I begin to realise the full significance of two related conditions of the context in which Chaucer wrote. First of all, there was no printing press and, secondly, he therefore wrote to be *heard* rather than to be read.

Historians and critics writing about Chaucer's life and times usually point this out. D S Brewer, for instance, quotes from Edward IV's Household Book:

> These Esquires of housold of old be accustomed, winter and summer, in afternoones and in eueninges, to drawe to Lordes Chambres within Court, there to keep honest company after there Cunninge, in talking of Cronicles of kinges, and of others Pollicies, or in pipeing or harpeing, synginges, or other actes marcealls, to helpe to occupie the Court, and accompanie estraingers, till the time require of departing.

and comments:

> These splendid, sophisticated courtly gatherings were the primary audience Chaucer had in mind for his poems and even his sermons, for the Miller's or Reeve's Tale as well as the Book of the Duchess and the Troilus. The famous Troilus frontispiece shows Chaucer at the height of his fame in the late 'eighties reading to the assembled Court. Doubtless it is an idealized picture, but . . . it reminds us that poetry in Chaucer's time was still mainly heard, not read; and that reading aloud was the primary means of 'publishing' for Chaucer.
>
> (*Chaucer*, London, 1973, pp. 27–28)

Yes, yes, very interesting, but I tended to ignore it because *they* may have heard it but I rarely did. I couldn't perform it myself and on the few occasions when someone did it for me I was hampered by a belief that I could never do the same and by being unable to keep up with the sense. Chaucer tended to stay firmly on the page for me, as black print, even though I knew that all poetry has to be sound to be fully alive.

All my conventional study of Chaucer tended to leave him on the page, too. Chaucer's verse belonged as much or more to an oral culture as to a written one but literary historical scholarship has to work through documentary evidence to catch an echo of the oral culture. Literary historical scholarship is itself a highly developed and sophisticated construct of a written culture. Its bias is towards what is written and what is read. This can lead to a misapprehension of the context and audience for Chaucer's verse. For instance, the manuscript analogues for the folk-tale used by the Pardoner have been exhaustively traced in many languages. At least one apparent echo of phrasing from a written form of it has been discerned in Chaucer's version. All this tends to give the impression of Chaucer borrowing from his reading to enrich his writing, as he undoubtedly did. However, it is a *folk*-tale that the Pardoner uses and by very definition the known written versions of it must be the very small tip of a huge and now invisible (and inaudible!) iceberg of word of mouth versions. Chaucer writes from an oral tradition; it is most likely that his first experience of that story was from a telling of it, not from his reading.

Scholars and critics know this but cannot change the materials with which they work and so the emphasis remains a little awry. In noting the existence of a character a little like the Pardoner in the *Roman de la rose* (which Chaucer is known to have read and written because he translated it), Coghill and Tolkien admit that that character 'Faux-Semblant, as his name implies, is no more than an idea on legs, a literary clothes-peg' (*The Pardoner's Tale*, London, 1958, p. 54). Chaucer's Pardoner is very different and certainly not founded on his reading. (On the other hand, we should not unimaginatively assume that he is the exact opposite: an attempt at a fully realistic and consistent portrait of a contemporary figure. There is much that falls in between, as I hope to indicate later.) He is created from life and his creation is much more in the folk, the oral and the performance tradition than it is in the literary one. Chaucer did go to Italy and learn from Dante and Boccaccio, but he quite possibly heard as much as he read of these two and they, as much as he, expected to be heard rather than read.

Nevertheless, study of Chaucer concentrates on the written. The student can find a great deal of interesting research and interpretation based on documents. This is fine but it doesn't get Chaucer off the page. Scholars and critics know that this must be done. They show it in their choice of phrasing:

There is one passage in which Chaucer *peeps* through the Pardoner more unmistakably, in a delicious rise into pure bathos;

listen to the growing climax of abomination that issues from gambling

(Coghill and Tolkien, p. 30)

For the whole homily as actually delivered to simple folk 'dwellyng upon lond' is not set down verbatim: part of it is reported, in satiric vein, to another kind of audience that is listening not so much to the homily as to the self-revelation. Let us say, merely for the sake of convenience, that the Pardoner fits his rural 'sermon' into an 'address' delivered to the Pilgrims. It is a *joy to watch* his off-hand ease at the job of conveying an exposition within an exposition. Into the 'prologe' which expounds his method to his present audience is woven a long quotation from a past *performance*

(G G Sedgwick, 'The Progress of Chaucer's Pardoner, 1880–1940', Chaucer: Modern Essays in Criticism, ed. E Wagenknecht, New York, 1959, p. 133)

(My emphasis in both cases)

The full implications of this oral context remain submerged, however, because a written culture is trying to expound an oral one. We, as the hard of hearing, are trying to understand the art of a partially sighted age!

The second example, from G G Sedgwick, does highlight the fact that of all Chaucer's works *The Pardoner's Tale* is one of the most oral, the most performed and the least intelligible unless heard and even seen. Chaucer used a tremendous range of styles within the deliberately flexible framework of *The Canterbury Tales*; some do move towards the 'literary' (the Knight's and the Parson's tales, for instance) but all were to be read aloud and the Pardoner's cries out for dramatic reading with the reader performing the part of the Pardoner and, through him, all the parts the Pardoner plays.

It is worth just noting how strongly the structure, language, rhythm and narrative technique of the verse implies that it should be spoken. The whole of the *Tales* is arranged like a play with actors who take centre stage in turn to tell their stories. In between tales they interrelate. Everything is spoken by a character; Chaucer even makes a character of himself as one of the pilgrims. The verse has a fluid and easy pace, avoiding a density which would be too much for a listener to follow. It is frequently rhetorical and dramatic in tone; using repetition, emphasis, exclamation, bathos and every other form of rhetoric for which Chaucer was admired in his own time and of which he was always in total control. It is important to remember that rhetoric was devised for oral persuasion. Chaucer's language is always appropriate, not only to its subject but to his audience. The Court, his first audience, like all courts, pretended to sophistication in language but understood and enjoyed the calling of a spade a spade. They were not separate from the folk tradition as a modern urban audience can be. They appreciated images like:

> I rekke nevere, whan that they been beryed,
> Though that hir soules goon a-blakeberyed!
>
> (ll.405–406)[1]

as well as more sophisticated vocabulary from the French which was the courtly language up to Chaucer's time. Finally, there is always a strong impression of a speaker who is consciously addressing the audience directly. The Pardoner addresses his country congregations:

> Goode men and wommen, o thyng warne I yow
>
> (l.377)

at the same time, his fellow-pilgrims:

> 'Goode men,' I seye, 'taak of my wordes keepe...'
>
> (l.352)

(where the 'I seye' is for them), and, through his care in making allowance for these audiences, he addresses us, through the narrator's ironic mediation. We are, or should be, in the same position as that third gathering — the court assembly who would listen to the reading of the tale.

All these are characteristic of a performed poetry. As I've said, though, *The Pardoner's Tale* is distinctively 'showy'.

First, the Pardoner himself is a showman. He's a vain performer, a charlatan, a trickster. We simply don't appreciate this properly unless his personality comes out in performance of the verse. Not that there is a lack of invitation to a performance.

---

[1] See 'A note on the text' (p. 8) regarding line references.

The Pardoner goes to some trouble to set up his audience, apparently inviting them to gather round at an 'alestake' while he makes a performance even of thinking 'Upon som honest thyng while that I drynke' (1.328). His description of his technique in gulling country congregations in his prologue is driven by his vanity. He can't stop at description, though, he has to perform. With that 'Goode men' at line 352 he slips from description into a performance of an extract from his habitual sermon. His vanity will not allow him restraint; he cannot believe that his audience won't appreciate and applaud his talent for clever preaching even if he has to admit that it is all dedicated to simple selfish greed on his part. He breaks off from the quotation at line 388, but he is still illustrating his techniques of performance:

> Thanne peyne I me to strecche forth the nekke,
> And est and west upon the peple I bekke,
> As dooth a dowve sittynge on a berne.
> Myne handes and my tonge goon so yerne
> That it is joye to se my bisynesse.
>
> (ll.395–399)

This cries out for the kind of dramatic reading an actor might perform. Some, to my mind rather over-literary, critics have cited the dove image as evidence of the Pardoner's impudence and pride because it implies he associates himself with the holy dove of peace. I think this misses the point that it is a farmyard image, a comic piece of mimicry which the audience will recognise instantly and want to see translated into action as the oral story-teller always tends to supplement verbal images with action. They'd be itching to make that jerking movement of the head and neck themselves. It is not surprising that I didn't find the sophisticated 'mental' and extended images that I so appreciated in modern literature, in Chaucer. His imagery, like his language, in a tale like this one, is immediate, physical, active.

When the Pardoner begins his tale and launches into his sermon against drink, swearing and gaming, he invites his audience of pilgrims willingly to suspend their disbelief (to adapt a phrase from Coleridge). This invitation comes in the form of the power and persuasiveness of his delivery. If we sometimes have difficulty persuading ourselves simply to accept the sermon regardless of what the preacher has already told us about himself, it is probably because we treat it too much as a written text and not as a performance. This is where the fact that I am writing an essay to be read lets me down, but try to put this into sound and action:

> The apostel wepyng seith full pitously,
> 'Ther walken manye of which yow toold have I —
> I seye it now wepyng, with pitous voys —
> They been enemys of Cristes croys,
> Of which the ende is deeth; wombe is hir god!'
> O wombe! O bely! O stynkyng cod,
> Fulfilled of donge and of corrupcioun!
> At either end of thee foul is the soun.
> How greet labour and cost is thee to fynde!
> Thise cookes, how they stampe, and streyne, and grynde,
> And turnen substaunce into accident
> To fulfille al thy likerous talent!
> Out of the harde bones knokke they
> The mary, for they caste noght awey
> That may go thurgh the golet softe and swoote.

(ll.528–543)

First the Pardoner takes the opportunity to quote from St Paul so that he can take on a part. Not only that but he tells how he plays the part (a hint of guidance from Chaucer to the performing reader): 'I seye it now wepyng, with pitous voys'. Then, having made full use of the quavering voice of emotion, he breaks into exclamation of a blunt and powerfully immediate and sensual kind, illustrating the physical consequences of gluttony in a way any audience can understand and relate to. Then he makes the calm and reasonable appeal to common self-interest by calling into question the expense and bother of it all, following this up with highly onomatopoeic, almost grunting, description of the efforts of cooks. This extract ends with the unpleasant sound of excessive consumption, suggesting nausea by the use of those final *s* sounds in combination with the word 'golet' which requires a paroxysm in the throat.

The Pardoner uses different voices all through his tale. As he comes to the end of his sermon, which has been dotted with quotation and varying voices and tones, he surprises the reader, although it would be no surprise to the hearer, by not simply quoting some biblical or classical authority but by taking on the parts of swearing gamesters:

> And forther over, I wol thee telle al plat
> That vengeance shal nat parten from his hous
> That of his othes is to outrageous.
> 'By Goddes precious herte,' and 'By his nayles,'
> And 'By the blood of Crist that is in Hayles,
> Sevene is my chaunce, and thyn is cynk and treye!'
> 'By Goddes armes, if thou falsly pleye,
> This daggere shal thurghout thyn herte go!'
>
> (ll.648–655)

and when he finally gets on to his tale of the three 'riotoures' he tells a great deal of it through the medium of dialogue. The Pardoner is an actor, who acts, in this case, to show how well he can act. He is therefore an excellent subject for dramatic rendition. The stage in his story where the two older 'riotoures' are left by the younger to give in to the evil suggestion of one of them is maybe not as subtle as Iago's temptation of Othello but it is at least as *theatrical* as Antonio's temptation of Sebastian in *The Tempest*. In both cases, one of the evil pair shows a not altogether psychologically convincing imperviousness to suggestion so that the full horror of that suggestion can be drawn out for the audience. When it is suggested that they could divide the treasure between them, the second man says innocently:

> 'I noot hou that may be.
> He woot that the gold is with us tweye;
> What shal we doon? What shal we to hym seye?'
>
> (ll.816–818)

The other parts available in the tale allow for a virtuoso range. As well as the three central characters there are the potboy and the taverner who would require contrasting voices and tones, the enigmatic and strangely calm old man, the 'pothecarie's' voice of doom and the blunt approach of the Host after the Pardoner has finished.

However, the need to read aloud or perform this tale is not just established by the fact that the Pardoner is a showman who uses rhetoric, folk-tale and preaching, which are all oral media, in a context of 'staged' story-telling. It is also called for by what Chaucer is doing in *his* tale. Chaucer handles the Pardoner ironically, satirising him. Ironic satire, or the statement of different or opposing meanings in one set of words in order to expose folly or sin, is frequently revealed by tone of voice. We tend to miss the satire in this tale unless we concentrate on spoken tone.

For instance, the major objection to *The Pardoner's Tale* comes in the form of questioning the psychological consistency of a crafty type like the Pardoner shamelessly revealing his trickery before his tale and then trying it on with the company of pilgrims at the end. I would argue, though, that this is only a problem if you are reading the tale like a novel. This prevents you accepting the tale on its own spoken terms. The truest comparison to a modern form is to television and radio satires like 'Spitting Image' and 'Week Ending'. In shows like these we accept a blatant type of parody in which an absurd and exaggerated figure of, say, a major politician is used to represent the truth behind the mask of public relations presentation. In such sketches these figures blatantly reveal what are meant to be the true motivations behind their actions. Our laughter at the Pardoner must be at his absurd action in performance; we accept his self-betrayal as part of an exaggerated satirical portrait.

There are other good accounts of the Pardoner's self-betrayal which treat him more as a realistic, psychologically consistent portrayal. If you are interested, have a look at G L Kittredge's 'Chaucer's Pardoner' (in *Chaucer: Modern Essays in Criticism*, ed. E Wagenknecht, New York, 1959) and the introduction to the Harrap edition of the tale, edited by Coghill and Tolkien (London, 1958) page 28. The interesting point in common for all of these is that they are *dramatic* interpretations. As soon as we read the tale aloud to get the effect of the psychology of immediate action rather than read it ponderously as written text, thus expecting the psychology of planned and considered action, the inconsistency is no longer perceived.

Chaucer may have been one of the first poets to *write* in English and literacy may have been one of the chief weapons in the hands of the ruling minority in church and state in his day. Nevertheless, in his hands English entered written verse form but remained spoken in tone and character. It is something like a transcription of a tape-recorded conversation: it has to be put back into sound to make full sense. Chaucer, like Shakespeare, did not have a modern concept of the sacrosanct literary text. When he broke off his writing of *The Canterbury Tales* he appended a 'retraccioun' in which he 'revoked' all his profane tales. For him, verse was either for entertainment or for moral instruction (or both). The latter he conceived in the form of sermons, 'broadcast', so to speak, to a congregation. The former was convivial, performed, a group activity. Unlike a modern *published* work of literature, Chaucer's poems resemble the texts of Shakespeare's plays, working documents which would be fleshed out in performance.

So, if I go back to my problems, I find that my difficulties with the language would have been lessened by reading and performing aloud; my sense of Chaucer's naïvety was due to my failure to realise the performance nature of what I was reading and its relation to its audience; and my perception of psychological inconsistency was due to my application of standards established in the modern novel.

The pen may be mightier than the sword, but language in action can be far mightier still than the written/read word. I am restricted here by writing an essay; it is unlikely that anyone will read it with as much conviction as I have written it. Words in performance carry far greater weight.

It only takes a few hours' work with those notes on pronunciation of Chaucer's English to be found in most editions of the tale. Read *The Pardoner's Prologue and Tale*, like all Chaucer's writing, aloud.

AFTERTHOUGHTS

1

Do you agree with Smith that 'all poetry has to be sound to be fully alive' (page 19)?

2

'We, as the hard of hearing, are trying to understand the art of a partially sighted age' (page 21). What does Smith mean by this?

3

Compare Smith's attitude towards consistency of characterisation (page 26) with that of Watts (pages 11–12).

4

Does Smith convince you in this essay that *The Pardoner's Prologue and Tale* is best read aloud?

Mark Spencer Ellis

Mark Spencer Ellis is Head of English at Forest School and a Chief Examiner in English A level for the London Examinations Board.

ESSAY

States of mind — action — moral judgement

What is an agreement? How do people arrive at it? Our conventional views of the interaction between different parties make these virtually non-questions. We all know how agreements come about, and we can all tell when what is called one is in fact a dominant person laying down the law to others. This is the assumption we bring to Chaucer's text and to the agreements struck in it.

> And thus acorded been thise shrewes tweye
> To sleen the thridde, as ye han herd me seye.
>
> (ll.835–836)[1]

But a glance at the previous lines raises questions about 'thus acorded'. Where is the discussion? In fact, 'thus' is more an indication of narrative pace than a demonstration of agreement. We are aware of a gap, a gap which our concept of narrative would fill with thought.

The first rioter's proposal of how to murder the youngest (ll.829–836) isn't so much a proposal as a statement. Agreement

---

[1] See 'A note on the text' (p. 8) regarding line references.

is automatic, and so is the consequent action. Exactly the same gap can be seen in line 802. 'That oon of hem the cut broghte in his fest' follows directly from the 'worste' (1.776) of them suggesting or advising ('Wherfore I rede', 1.793) a course of action. No discussion follows; the plan is put into action the very moment it is articulated. Even the original oath which the three rioters take to kill Death is sworn the instant it is proposed:

> Togidres han thise thre hir trouthes plight
> To lyve and dyen ech of hem for oother

(ll.702–703)

The pace is stressed by the way in which 'Plight' picks up the rhyme 'night', the last word of the rioter's suggestion:

> He shal be slayn, he that so manye sleeth,
> By Goddes dignitee, er it be nyght!

(ll.700–701)

We are allowed no pause at the end of the verse paragraph. Any expectation we might have entertained about the other two rioters thinking about the idea or even stating their agreement is blown away in the vigour of the second half of the couplet.

This aspect of *The Pardoner's Tale* presents an immediate challenge to the contemporary reader. The assumptions we bring to our reading of narrative include ideas about 'character' which are difficult to square with the demands of the text. ('Character' is in inverted commas because the more we examine the prologue and tale, the more we become aware of how inappropriate it is to approach a fourteenth-century text without reassessing our prejudices about the relationship between the individual and society, and whether our ideas about independent thought and decision-taking can remain viable.) The rioters never stop to think, they never discuss what makes them 'acorded'.

One possible reading is that they are so fixed in their selfishness and acquisitiveness that they don't bother to pause. This interpretation would preserve the comforting (to us) idea that thought and decision-taking remain as realistic options — for other people if not for the rioters — and that this capacity is central to what constitutes our idea of a human being. However, this is not the only form of gap which is found in the tale.

A tale tells a story. That seems simple enough but *The*

Pardoner's Tale presents us with surprises if we extend this assumption and expect the narrative to centre on the actual events. Most noticeable is that we are never allowed to engage our imagination with the climax:

> What nedeth it to sermone of it moore?
> For right as they hadde cast his deeth bifoore
> Right so they han hym slayn, and that anon.
>
> (ll.879–881)

The first line draws attention to the narrative voice, to the Pardoner. The control he exercises undermines the scope of our imaginative entering into the story. We are made aware of our role as listeners. Then the tense shifts into the pluperfect. 'Hadde' and 'han' distance the events; to visualise them we need to push our memories back some seventy lines:

> Looke whan that he is set, that right anoon
> Arys as though thou woldest with hym pleye,
> And I shal ryve hym thurgh the sydes tweye
> Whil that thou strogelest with hym as in game,
> And with thy daggere looke thou do the same
>
> (ll.826–830)

The idea of the murder is presented here as a proposition; the force of the narrative for the contemporary reader is on whether the second rioter will agree, but for the fourteenth century the relationship between state of mind and action is much more immediate. We are effectively distanced from a reading of this climax which would allow as to dwell on the event itself.

The reading and teaching of nineteenth- and twentieth-century fiction has fostered a totally different approach. When discussing or criticising such texts students are encouraged to look at events and then to speculate as to why they happened. This speculation centres on characters, their motives, and, central to this issue, why they chose to do as they did. Events which follow each other more quickly than realism allows are read as comic; indeed they form the staple of cartoons. Characters who don't 'think' are not worth serious consideration, are two-dimensional. This form of critical approach has been so dominant that it's possible to find whole volumes of essays on Shakespeare plays which treat them as if they should be read as novels about 'characters'. This will not do. Not for Shakespeare but in particular not for Chaucer. *The Pardoner's Prologue and Tale* first challenges our conventional notions about character and events, and then, perhaps more disturbingly, undermines some fundamental assumptions about social morality.

When the Pardoner produces the examples of Lot and Herod to illustrate the terrible results of drunkenness, the state of mind and the action are linked as briskly as they are in the examples listed above:

> Lo, how that dronken Looth, unkyndely,
> Lay by his doughtres two, unwityngly;
> So dronke he was, he nyste what he wroghte.
>
> (ll.485–487)

Although the interpretation of this episode which sees it as a dreadful example of drunken double incest is an alteration of an older reading which saw the daughters heroically prepared to continue their family by the only available means, what is relevant to this essay's argument is the juxtaposition of the act (l.486) and the state (l.487). Even if we accept the common medieval gloss which finds the story appalling, the way the Pardoner gives us the example expressly cuts out the option of our imagining Lot *choosing* to sin when drunk. The same applies to Herod's order for the beheading of John the Baptist:

> Whan he of wyn was repleet at his feeste,
> Right at his owene table he yaf the heeste
> To sleen the Baptist John, ful giltelees.'
>
> (ll.489–491)

Again, there is no thought or choice involved — in marked contrast with the biblical account (Matthew 14:12; Mark 6:26) where Herod is all too aware of the trap he has fallen into. In the Pardoner's world 'the heeste' (l.490) is waiting only for drunkenness to explode on the guiltless John.

It is not only the idea of individual choice which is undermined in the tale. The very concept of the individual person is subjected to a severe battering. Take the first or 'proudeste' (l.716) rioter. There are two moments when his speech can be read as a monument of self-assertion. 'Look at me; take notice of what I am saying; my words are going to cause events.' The first passage has to be quoted in full to illustrate this:

> Thise riotoures thre of which I telle,
> Longe erst er prime rong of any belle,
> Were set hem in a taverne to drynke,
> And as they sat, they herde a belle clynke
> Biforn a cors, was caried to his grave.
> That oon of hem gan callen to his knave:
> 'Go bet,' quod he, 'and axe redily
> What cors is this that passeth heer forby;
> And looke that thou reporte his name weel.'
>
> (ll.661–669)

The gratuitous warning of line 669 stresses the way in which the rioter presents himself as instigator, as responsible for the momentum of the boy. However, this self-assertion is in response to the invasion of their world by the sound of the passing-bell. The rioters' sense of confidence is suggested in line 663 where the regular iambic rhythm of the previous couplet moves into a line which asks to be read as three closely linked sections, culminating in the purpose 'to drynke'. The sense requires a pause. The rioters have organised themselves to this end. But the verse moves on to the second half of the couplet where the sinister 'clynke' disturbs the settled mood. There is no punctuation at the end of line 664, so only the briefest of pauses which doesn't allow us (or the rioters) to ponder this unnerving juxtaposition of drinking and death; we move on to the uncompromising image of the funeral. So the vigour of the rioter's orders is an attempt to seize back the narrative initiative, to be in charge of events.

The wind is taken completely out of his sails by the response of the boy:

> 'Sire,' quod this boy, 'it nedeth never-a-deel;
> It was me toold er ye cam heer two houres.'
>
> (ll.670–671)

Even though the rioter's bluster concludes at the end of a verse paragraph, the demands of the couplet do not allow the narrative to pause when he has finished talking; 'weel' (l.669) requires a rhyme, and when it comes it is devastating. The verbal vigour achieved nothing, the order was unnecessary, and the boy did not move. The extent of this deflation is further pointed by the rioter's silence when the boy has finished speaking. His final words are a moral couplet, a complete end to his speech:

> Beth redy for to meete hym everemoore;
> Thus taughte me my dame; I sey namoore.

(ll.683–684)

A full stop at the end of a couplet which is the end of a speech. Even if the last three words hadn't been such a decisive signing-off, it would be clear that the space was there to be exploited, for the rioter to make another attempt to assert himself. However, his silence is pointed by the way in which the space is filled by a new speaker, 'this taverner' (l.685), who supports everything the boy said.

The second time this happens is even more spectacular. On meeting the old man the rioter comes out with a particularly stinging insult:

> Why lyvestow so longe in so greet age?

(l.719)

The rhetorical question is designed to prompt applause from his followers. It is cutting, clever and, in its own terms, unanswerable. The question is also an emphatically public one; it is for the benefit of the other two rioters, it is to show who is in charge. The immediate answer breaks the rules of the question. A logical reply is not what a rhetorical question requires. The effect is to remove the initiative for a second devastating moment away from the person who is attempting vigorous self-assertion.

> This olde man gan looke in his visage,
> And seyde thus: 'For I ne kan nat fynde
> A man, though that I walked into Ynde,
> Neither in citee ne in no village,
> That wolde chaunge his youthe for myn age'

(ll.720–724)

As the old man goes on to describe his state, the more the norms of conventional judgement are undermined. The constant wandering can only be ended by a decision which no one can make. It isn't possible to choose to exchange youth for age; the will or motivation behind the situation cannot be found in the human mind. 'Goddes wille' (l.726) is one area of responsibility but in the next line:

> Ne Deeth, allas, ne wol nat han my lyf.
>
> (l.727)

suggests that death is not an agent of God but an alternative power. 'Thus' which starts the next line serves to stress the helplessness of the individual to alter the course of events once his or her state — in this case, old age — is settled.

As on the other occasion when the rioter's attempt to browbeat his servant falls flat, so here it is the lack of response which shows his helplessness. The first verse paragraph in the old man's speech ends with a couplet:

> But yet to me she wol nat do that grace,
> For which ful pale and welked is my face.
>
> (ll.737–738)

This wraps up the statement which answers both of the rioter's questions: line 719 already quoted above, and the previous one:

> Why artow al forwrapped save thy face?
>
> (l.718)

The opportunity is there for the rioter to step in and retake the initiative. He doesn't. The old man continues, and rebukes him for his bad manners, for attempting to break the code of social behaviour:

> Agayns an oold man, hoor upon his heed,
> Ye sholde arise.
>
> (ll.743–744)

The futility of these attempts is disturbing because they threaten the basic assumptions about characters which are deeply rooted in our twentieth-century view of what distinguishes an individual. However unpleasant the rioter may be, at least he is attempting to be different from anybody else. But in the fourteenth century, as Stephen Knight succinctly puts it:

> The medieval idea of the person (ontology) depended on a quite different, indeed reverse, notion, namely that people

were primarily social and only in aberrance or in transition would be individual.[2]

The way in which the rioter's wish to be an individual is denied sweepingly by the narrative has implications which go beyond his particular fate. What defines him is not the sum of individual characteristics but his role and state of mind. The three of them are called rioters before we have seen them indulging in any rioting. They are not given any names by which to distinguish themselves. Reading today's works, we expect the names of characters to be among the first pieces of information we should be given. This is not so with Chaucer; his writing reflects a different attitude to individuality. For example, when names are supplied, they tend to come at the end of a description of the character's social behaviour and function. In *The General Prologue* we are only given two: the Prioress's, 'Eglentyne' (1.121) which is a reflection of her choosing a name suggestive of beauty rather than piety, and the Friar's, 'Huberd' (1.269) which comes in the very last line about him. The same can be seen in *The Franklin's Tale*, a work which attracts considerable critical attention because it can be read as an examination of how individuals *as* individuals come to terms with the sort of problems which arise from the feelings of different and unique people. Rather disturbingly for such a twentieth-century reading, the names of the three principals are held back until their behaviour has been described in detail, in the cases of Arveragus and Dorigen almost 100 lines after they enter the story.

It is not just the concept of innate individuality which this text undermines. *The Pardoner's Prologue and Tale* goes much further than that in its capacity to destabilise whole views about society. The central ideas of what constitutes 'good' and 'bad' behaviour are brought into sharp relief when we look at the relationship between the Pardoner and his audience.

The language he uses suggests a clear structure of social morality. The 'gentils' (1.323) ask for 'som moral thyng' (1.325), and he settles down to ponder what is 'honest' (1.328). His abiding theme is a 'moral' tag:

---

[2] Stephen Knight, *Geoffrey Chaucer (Rereading literature)* (Oxford, 1986), p. 126.

Radix malorum est Cupiditas

(1.334)

There is a certainty with which judgemental labels are attached to social behaviour: 'defaute' (1.370), 'synne horrible' (1.379) are assumed to be self-explanatory. Abstract terms are used with enormous confidence; the ethical structure of the prologue and tale depends on our having no doubts about the meaning and relevance of such terms as 'avarice', 'cursedness', 'hoolynesse', 'coveitise', 'folye', 'lecherye', 'glotonye', 'vileynye', 'vice', 'honour', 'dishonour' or 'wikkednesse'. However, when we look at the context in which they are applied, we can see that far from being ethical absolutes these terms are highly contingent; they depend on the circumstances in which they are offered as judgemental descriptions.

The relationship the Pardoner establishes with his audience, indeed the only relationship which allows the reader to feel comfortable, sets up an alternative scale of values. Good and Bad, Right and Wrong are not concepts to be disputed; they are simply ignored as the Pardoner creates his own poles of judgement. These are the simple substitution of Quick-witted and Gullible as the two extremes. He disarms the audience by removing the possibility of ethical disapproval. The key terms he uses set up an alternative 'morality'; his is the world of the joke: 'gaude' (1.389), 'japes' (1.394). Disapproval is difficult because he has decided the rules. To set oneself up against the Pardoner is to break the relationship in which he is sharing with us the tricks of his trade. Those who are his victims are held up to be laughed at by us as well:

> Relikes been they, as wenen they echoon.

(1.349)

He encourages our acquiescing laughter with the throwaway lines:

> I rekke nevere, whan that they been beryed,
> Though that hir soules goon a-blakeberyed.

(ll.405–406)

However, the vanity — identifying with the clever rather than with the gullible — which may lead the audience to accept these values is itself destabilised the moment the relationship with the Pardoner seems to be established:

> I wol noon of the apostles countrefete;
> I wol have moneie, wolle, chese, and whete,
> Al were it yeven of the povereste page,
> Or of the povereste wydwe in a village,
> Al sholde hir children sterve for famyne.
> Nay, I wol drynke licour of the vyne
> And have a joly wenche in every toun.

(ll.447–453)

This passage never allows us to feel that we can bring a settled response to the Pardoner. The first line is an assertion which follows from his alternative ethical code. The apostles are rejected as a rule-book rather than as individuals. The vigorous acquisitiveness of 'I wol have' follows logically from his cleverness; this is the aim. The 'povereste page' is therefore a legitimate target, lacking the wits to build up his own possessions. The next two lines present a problem. The 'povereste wydwe' is the conventional image of what deserves charity, and therefore to set her up as a victim simply stresses the Pardoner's standards. But if we find ourselves laughing with him, the image of the dead children brings us up short. It is shocking but it is also a legitimate object of laughter if we have embraced the Pardoner's values. The assertive claim which follows, and which completes the couplet, is not a contradiction if we really do go along with the division of humankind into those who deserve to win and those who deserve to lose. The final line presents a further problem. It demands that we accept the Pardoner as he projects himself, and yet the clear implications in *The General Prologue* about his homosexuality and lack of the necessary quipment to make good his boast make us draw back. This passage shows how we are never given the opportunity to look at the Pardoner from a settled viewpoint. To disapprove of him is to identify with his victims, to brand oneself not as moral but as stupid. But to go along with the world of 'gaudes' and 'japes' is to regard dead babies as a joke.

What is a joke, what is serious? The polarity is set up but there is no fixed point where the audience can sense firm ground. The pace of the narrative is disconcerting. Nobody walks or strolls; the rioters 'stirte' (1.705) and 'ran' (1.768), as did the youngest of them (1.869). 'Anon' figures in the narrative frequently, for example in lines 477, 511, 805, 826, 864 and 888. As has already been suggested, this implies a cartoon-like story, one of responses which are so immediate that they cannot be taken seriously. However, if the pace is to be seen in the context of medieval ideas about the relationship between state of mind and action, then the effect is a disturbing one. Rather than seeing these events as absurd or as the activities of two-dimensional characters, we are bound to view them as illustrations of the helplessness of the human lot, of our inability to dictate either the direction or the pace of our lives.

This uncertainty also undermines the confident tone of the judgements. All the clear abstract terms which imply no doubts about what is right and what is wrong are based in 'auctoritee'. The Bible is frequently cited as the authority behind such judgements:

> The hooly writ take I to my witnesse.
>
> (1.483)

is only the first mention of a prop which supports the examples the Pardoner produces. Adam's fate is 'as I rede' (1.508); 'victories' can be found 'in the Olde Testament' (1.575), and if any doubt remains, 'Looketh the Bible' (1.578). Although this is the most frequently quoted authority, 'Witnesse on Mathew' (1.634), 'seith the hooly Jeremye' (1.635), the simple fact of something being written down is enough to give it the necessary status; 'as the book seith us' (1.622) gives authority to the story of Demetrius. A world which pays such regard to authority simply as authority is vulnerable once the moral absolutes on which that authority is based are shown to be arbitrary. The Bible, on the face of it, seems a reasonable basis of morality but in the fourteenth century it cannot be separated from the immense political and economic power of the Church. And it is from the Church that the Pardoner derives his legitimacy:

> ...the auctoritee
> Which that by bulle ygraunted was to me.
>
> (ll.387–388)

His performance starts with establishing his credentials:

> ...my bulles shewe I, alle and some.
> Our lige lordes seel on my patente

(1.336–337)

To challenge the Pardoner is to risk upsetting one of the most powerful institutions in the country. No wonder he is at pains to stress this authority.

When we come to the end of the tale the invitation to the pilgrims to approach and pay for the chance to revere the 'relikes' is doubly disturbing. First, we don't believe him. He has taken us into his confidence and told us that they are false relics. This, however, leaves the assumption that somewhere, somewhere else, there must be true relics, and that they really do 'work'. (The same applies to the bulls he exhibits; that they may be fakes doesn't remove the awareness that there are pardoners with 'genuine' authority.) But if this is so, why isn't it obvious? What kind of a religion is it which reveals itself through supernatural interventions in human affairs but is vulnerable to confidence-tricksters? The second problem is to do with the very nature of authority. It is in the name of the Church that the Pardoner issues his invitation:

> Boweth youre heed under this hooly bulle!

(1.909)

Medieval people questioned the authority of the Church only at the risk of death. Yet when authority is seen to be so capable of manipulation, the whole concept of an absolute moral structure to society has to be questioned.

The term 'fals' is particularly interesting in this context. It is introduced by the Host, commenting on *The Physician's Tale*:

> This was a fals cherl and a fals justise.

(1.289)

To describe a justice as 'fals' suggests that this is, naturally enough, as opposed to a true one. But the 'cherl' is simply wicked. 'Fals' is not a judgement which can be slotted neatly into a moral framework. When the Pardoner congratulates himself on his 'false japes' (1.394) the term is a tautology. There cannot be 'true' japes; and in his amoral world 'fals' is a congratulatory term. In the same way it is a sign of his cleverness that anyone who opposes him won't get away without being 'defamed falsly' (1.415). The word is ceasing to fit into a moral code. 'Fals sweryng (1.632) is simply a step further than 'Gret sweryng' (1.631), and, as with the example in line 415, a 'false empoysonere' (1.894) doesn't indicate someone who only pretends to poison his companions. So what are we to make of it when 'mankynde' (1.900) is proclaimed to be 'so fals and so unkynde' (1.903)?

If absolute morality as put forward by the Church is not a satisfactory basis for deciding the force of 'fals', then the answer is provided in two words which are specifically linked with it. Death, for the rioters, is 'this false traytour' (1.699). Again, in line 753, Death is 'thilke traytour'. A traitor is someone who attempts to destroy the prevailing social order. Even now the title has sinister overtones, especially when one considers what penalty most social groupings decide is appropriate for treachery. But in drawing attention to the arbitrary nature of the Church's authority, the Pardoner is prompting his audience to thoughts which would qualify every one of them for the label of traitor.

The other word is even more revealing. In accusing the old man of being in league with Death, the rioter addresses him as 'thou false theef' (1.759). What is being stolen?

> Ther cam a privee theef men clepeth Deeth
>
> (1.675)

Everything, even life itself, is property. It is the reward of cleverness and what is vulnerable to thieves.

The entire ethical structure of *The Pardoner's Prologue and Tale* is founded on this simple assumption. The illustrations he produces in the first half of the tale are hardly shining examples of worthy behaviour. With the dubious exception of Samson (1.555) they are all terrible warnings of how what the Church designates 'sin' can have enormous practical disadvantages. The 'wise philosophre' (1.620) Stilboun is simply advocating practical self-interest. 'Attilla, the grete conquerour' (1.579) is cited because drunkenness put an end to his career of rape and pillage. 'Morality' doesn't enter into it.

The promises which are implicit in the relics which the Pardoner offers are essentially practical and acquisitive:

> He that his hand wol putte in this mitayn,
> He shal have multipliyng of his grayn

(ll.373–374)

Lines 352–360 offer a universal vaccination against any known disaster which may threaten one's livestock. While this may seem a straightforward enough point, what is important is that the Pardoner, a man who knows his target audience all too well, hasn't mistaken the prevailing interests and standards.

There are no choices to be made. The 'moral vocabulary' suggests that there are, but the narrative makes it clear that our fate is decided by our state of mind, by our life-style.

> And right anon thanne comen tombesteres
> Fetys and smale, and yonge frutesteres

(ll.477–478)

The 'tombesteres' and 'frutesteres' have not been summoned. They are the natural result of the rioters' life-style. The cartoon-like vigour of the rioters' actions:

> Thus seyde this olde man;
> And everich of thise riotoures ran
> Til he cam to that tree . . .

(ll.767–769)

illustrates the inescapable result of their values. We cannot dismiss them as 'shallow' characters inhabiting an 'unreal' world. They are intensely disturbing, and the directness of the link between state of mind and action is spelled out in the activities of the youngest of them. He doesn't hatch the plot for himself; it arises fully formed in his mind through the agency of 'the feend' (l.844). And it is stressed that the state of mind is what led to the plan:

> For-why the feend foond hym in swich lyvynge
> That he hadde leve him to sorwe brynge.

(ll.847–848)

Permission? This raises questions about what sort of supreme arbiter or authority we ultimately have to face.

The final and most disturbing aspect of *The Pardoner's Prologue and Tale* is that the text does not simply undermine concepts such as individuality (from a twentieth-century view-point in particular), and authority. It also sets up an alternative which is shockingly unthinkable. If cleverness is the only virtue and material possessions the only reward worth striving for, what 'standards' are left?

When the Pardoner is called on to tell a tale, the framework the Host suggests is specifically one which is free from morality; indeed, it is this which prompts the 'gentils' to request an alternative, 'som moral thyng' (l.325):

> Telle us som myrthe or japes right anon.
>
> (l.319)

The natural world of the Pardoner is also that of the rioters. They have no time for questions of right and wrong; things are measured by their capacity to provoke laughter and provide pleasure. The advent of the 'tombesteres' and 'frutesteres' (l.477–488) stems from the rioters' laughter:

> And ech of hem at otheres synne lough.
>
> (l.476)

Happiness is:

> In myrthe and joliftee oure lyf to lyven
>
> (l.780)

and the youngest, contemplating the results of murdering his fellows, senses that no one 'sholde lyve so murye as I' (l.843). The final words of the first rioter are a celebration of self-indulgence; the rhyme points to the dismissal of any possible moral considerations:

> 'Now lat us sitte and drynke, and make us merie,
> And afterward we wol his body berie.'
>
> (ll.883–884)

The concluding paragraph of the text provides a 'solution' to the stormy confrontation between Pardoner and Host. It was the latter who invited the Pardoner to speak, and he who asked for 'japes'. *The Pardoner's Prologue and Tale* are uncompromising in their illustration of a world which cannot see anything except as a joke or 'gaude'. This is the only and the natural extension of a materialistic and acquisitive society which pays lip-service to a 'Christian' moral code. The Pardoner's state prompts the very same response when 'al the peple lough' (l.961) as that which signals the self-regarding amorality of the rioters in line 476. When the Knight asks the Pardoner to 'be glad and myrie of cheere' (l.963) and suggests that the whole company of pilgrims should return to the state when 'as we diden, lat us laughe and pleye' (l.967), his words acknowledge that the framework through which the Pardoner views the world is the only one with any practical application. This view is amoral, sees characters as two-dimensional, presents narrative as an animated cartoon, and is deadly serious.

AFTERTHOUGHTS

What problems for the twentieth-century reader of *The Pardoner's Prologue and Tale* are highlighted in this essay?

Compare Spencer Ellis's discussion of Chaucer's use of names (page 36) with the arguments put forward in the essay by Read (page 56).

What significance does Spencer Ellis attach to the use of the word 'fals' (pages 40–41)?

What are the implications of the final sentence of this essay (page 44)?

Charles Moseley

Charles Moseley teaches English at Cambridge University and at the Leys School, Cambridge. He is the author of numerous critical studies.

ESSAY

The cosmic banana-skin: the Pardoner v. his tale

Like that of the Wife of Bath, *The Pardoner's Tale* is preceded by a very long monologue where the self-satisfied and self-confident garrulousness of the characters tells us a great deal about them which is by no means to their credit. The Pardoner, with enormous energy, reveals not only his mean tricks in his disreputable profession but also his innermost motives, his utter contempt for his usual audience, and his cynical disregard of some of the most serious doctrines of the Church he supposedly serves. In either case, after such introductions, the tales that follow read very oddly indeed: though each will stand on its own, of course, as respectively a perfectly decent small romance and an excellent sermon, and can — perhaps, for a time, should — be so read, set in these particular mouths they raise awkward and uncomfortable questions.

In Chaucer's day and for long after, pardoners as a group had an appalling reputation as frauds, con men, libertines and drunkards. It is therefore no surprise that the picture of the Pardoner in the *General Prologue* runs true to this type and

Chaucer clearly expects his audience to regard him with revulsion. What is unusual is that the con man, in the prologue to the tale, is made to extend the sketch of the *General Prologue* by a detailed confession of his attitudes and tricks which, despite the surface courtesy of his address, puts up two fingers to the rest of the pilgrims who clearly disapprove of him and are nervous of the Host's selection of him for the next story, expecting him to scandalise them with immoral talk. In every sense, he simply could not care less.

His prologue is a masterpiece of black comedy. The self-satisfied description of what is a grotesque perversion of great abilities — eloquence, energy, wit, intelligence — is undercut throughout the prologue by passing references to what true religion and virtue are really like: the poverty and selflessness of the apostles (and Chaucer's Parson) which he rejects, the real concern for the spiritual welfare of his hearers that he casually disregards, the real holiness of relics and miracles that he blasphemes, the real power of God which he ignores but which he uses to frighten others. He is a mirror-image of all that is good, and his evil is focused in his blasphemous use of his power as a preacher. The picture he gives of himself performing in the pulpit, waving his arms in the elegant manner then admired, the false wolf in sheep's clothing against whom Christ himself warned us, is suddenly completely upstaged by the comparison of himself to a dove on a barn roof. The Dove of the Holy Spirit, reduced by him to an illustrative woodpigeon, is indeed near at hand, and may be using him in a way of which he could have no conception — as we shall see. And the implied similarity between his speech and the venom of the reptile which symbolised the devil in Eden (ll.413, 421)[1] reveals his true nature, in which he takes a ghastly pride.

This constant ironic valuing completely undercuts for us his self-confidence, his pride, his condescension and his impudence. For evil, as St Augustine pointed out, is nothing of itself: it is a perversion, a deprivation, of good, and those who commit themselves to it, who refuse to do God's work, become his tools. They may pretend they are free and independent, but their very

---

[1] See 'A note on the text' (p. 8) regarding line references.

continuance in being depends on their being sustained by the very Power they deny. The Pardoner is sawing off the branch on which he sits, and we are listening to a soul that is damned and does not yet know it.

The Pardoner has a lot of pride in his technical skill both as preacher and — it amounts to the same thing in him — as villain (ll.329ff, 341ff, 395ff, 915). He is amusedly aware that though a 'ful vicious man', he can stir men to real emotion and a devotion he despises. His contempt for his 'lewed' audience (ll.377ff, 437ff) reveals itself in the way he regards them as a mere lump — he uses a singular verb for the plural audience in line 392 — and the way he seems to absolve them indiscriminately as a group (ll.385ff) from the terrible pains of the purgatory in which they (and Chaucer's audience) believe. Impudently, he seems to assume — despite the clear evidence to the contrary — an equal cynicism in the pilgrim audience; his intimate and conspiratorial tone implies that they must share his contempt for his victims and his admiration for himself. This impudence grows from overweening pride and a refusal to see things as they really are — for example, his appearance suggests that he is, so to speak, cut off from all possibility of normal sexuality, yet he claims to be lecherous and a womaniser, and his roguery may in fact, by stirring feelings of real devotion, be doing the 'Cristes holy werk' to which he refers so sarcastically. He is open about his rapacity, his lust for power and his desire to deprive others of what they really need (l.448) purely for the delight in possession — avarice, like that of the rogues in his tale, in its pure form. There is therefore a progression in his evil, from pride (love for his own power), to envy (desire to take away the good of others), to anger and hatred (when he revenges himself on those who have hurt him, and cares nothing for the damnation of those he has misled). This results in a downward spiral of wallowing in the sins of lechery, gluttony and avarice. His avarice has lost even the bad excuse of a desire to satisfy his own needs; by his own admission he pursues it for its own sake, and his career has become a repetitive, useless treadmill. Sin is its own punishment, and he is locked in the prison of his own hell, constantly feeding afresh the flames of his own pride, envy, avarice and impotent lechery. The eunuch's physical sterility outwardly typifies the inner despair, the deepest blasphemy.

The most evil and most guilty man on the pilgrimage and in his own described world is nevertheless surrounded by the play of many ironies. First, there is the obvious fact that this monster offers to others a pardon which, if they are sincere in repentance, is genuine and would free them from guilt. But that is a freedom he can never know; every time he offers pardon with the motives he does, he increases his own guilt, and the victims he despises come out better than he does in the end. In him Chaucer underlines the self-destructiveness of sin, and the nature of a universe, a divine comedy, where the mercy of God can work even through the deepest and most unrepentant evil.

The major ironies, however, focus round the sermon he preaches and its situation. It is, of course, possible to read it simply as a magnificently told story, and detach it from its context. But this is to miss a great deal of its force. In the first place, it is quite specifically a sermon and needs to be heard as that. For the first audiences — both the imagined audience on the road to Canterbury, and the group to whom Chaucer might have read his work — would recognise it as a splendid example of a very well defined genre with its own conventions, rhetorical organisation, and expectations. With consummate skill — and daring confidence — Chaucer follows its initial vivid glimpse of the tavern where the three rogues are busy indulging in a whole complex of vices, by immediately, just as we are becoming interested, building up extraordinary suspense with the long discussion of drunkenness and blasphemy. This could have gone badly wrong, losing the audience before the story had got going, but it does not; it never ceases to hold our interest, with its little anecdotes, and vivid characterisations, and its tone ranging from the comical imitation of a drunkard's laboured snoring to grand and impressive warnings of the wrath of God. Then, the introduction of the haunting figure of the old man, whom we as listeners see is someone much more important than the three rogues realise, brings us powerfully back to the narrative of the story that will exemplify the themes the long digression opened up. The rapidity and economy of the narrative close in the final picture of the three corpses at the foot of a Tree of Death: a powerful visual symbol, for the bread and poisoned wine of the feast of unbrotherliness parody the saving Bread and Wine of the Mass, the rite of reconciliation and Life. Such a narrative, and such a handling of it, remain in the mind long after we have read it: exactly as a sermon should, it attaches a genuine feeling of horror to the abstract moral concepts of the sins that are its subject. We can, therefore, both be affected by it as a sermon — which we would be if we heard it without the prologue — and watch the skill with which we are being affected: Chaucer certainly expected us to do both, and the latter is just what the Pardoner is setting out to demonstrate as a matter of personal pride.

But among the expectations of sermons is an understanding of the relationship between the preacher and his material. Bringing this into play creates a massive irony. The preacher was supposed to pray for, and assumed to receive, the guidance of the Holy Spirit before he opened his mouth, but this man is preaching an excellent sermon with no such thought, purely to separate his victims from their money. He introduces it specifically as an example to illustrate his own skill in doing this:

> For though myself be a ful vicious man,
> A moral tale yet I yow telle kan,
> Which I am wont to preche for to wynne.

(ll.459–461)

Furthermore, this is not the only sermon preached in *The Canterbury Tales*; the Parson, a model of what a good and selfless priest should be, preaches another, and comparison of the two, and their effects, is inevitable. This raises the awkward question that the sermon preached from the very worst motives by a villain is far better, and far more conducive to true devotion, than the careful analysis of the Seven Deadly Sins preached in humility and devotion by a saint who refuses — a fine irony, considering he is himself a fiction — to tell a story. (A story is, after all, at best illusion and literally speaking a lie, and the Parson is quite properly refusing to deal with anything but ultimate truth.) Nobody ever wished *The Parson's Tale* a line longer, yet he ought to be the one to whom we listen most carefully. That we do not, that we find the Pardoner's narrative and personality so fascinating, suggests something about ourselves which is uncomfortable. We may know the truth and know the good, but evil is far more interesting to our fallen minds even when we know it is evil. In our fallen state, Chaucer seems to suggest, reason and knowledge will not lead us to goodness, but the emotional response to a good story just might.

There are further ironies generated by the context. Preached by a man who gulps a drink and gobbles a cake before he starts, it is a very effective tirade against drunkenness and gluttony. Preached by a man for whom money is everything, it demonstrates and attacks the destructive power of avarice. And so the themes of the sermon that the Pardoner told as an example of his 'craft' — Chaucer's word — are exemplified not only in the gluttonous, blasphemous, avaricious, murderous figures in the illustrative story in the tale — which normal assumptions about how a sermon should be organised would make us expect — but also are manifested most vividly and explicitly by its preacher. Unwittingly, he becomes the example in a sermon he did not mean to preach, and his tale turns round and bites him. But his sermon is also preached, as example or not, before an audience of pilgrims who are in the main little better than they should be. The Knight, the Parson, the Clerk and the Plowman are of course ideal figures, and no criticism is breathed of them; but all the others manifest in some degree the sins the Pardoner discusses. The members of the Brotherhood have brought their tame, drunken, cook with them, the Franklin thinks more of food than anything else, the Shipman, the Sergeant, the Merchant are all, it is hinted, far too unscrupulously concerned with money, and the Shipman is little better than a pirate; the Monk and the Prioress have very far from renounced the world as their profession demanded, and their sinfulness only looks better than that of the Pardoner himself because it is masked by good manners, pleasant address, and social status. The list of sinners could be extended, and the sermon preached ostensibly as an example in fact turns its guns — and we may be sure the Pardoner knew it — on its pilgrim audience. For the Pardoner is the great unmasker — not least of himself. He accepted the prissy misgivings about himself of the 'gentils' (l.324ff) and then, telling them a 'moral thyng', suggests implicitly that they deserve and are fit audience for the sermon he delivers. Moreover, he assumes as if it is beyond argument that they are interested in his profession and will rejoice in his techniques and share his contempt for his victims and for the very religion he appears to serve. His whole confession implied, indeed, by the very fact of being made in this bravura way, that the 'gentils' are as bad as he is, and his story compounds the insult. The socially acceptable Physician told a revolting and hamfisted tale which everybody thought a moral one; the revolting Pardoner now tells a story that really is moral, but his ending of it in a quarrel with the Host and the general laughter that ensues suggest that the moral is quite lost on his hearers: their reaction demonstrates the very moral blindness the Pardoner assumed in them and which they would, if challenged, have strenuously denied.

The final example of the Pardoner's contempt for his pilgrim audience comes as he reaches the grand climax of his peroration. He reminds them — the word 'thus' (1.915) sends us back to his introductory promise of a sermon 'which I am wont to preche, for to wynne' (1.461) — that he is a fraud and his sermon a means of cheating. Then, breathtakingly, he has the sheer brass neck to try his tricks on them even though he knows they know they are tricks — offering them his relics to kiss, offering them pardon, all for money, in a sort of Dutch auction. This must be an attempt at the acme of the con man's skill, to introduce yourself as a con man and get someone to give you his wallet. It is very funny as long as it isn't your wallet, and it is surprising how many people fall for it. As far as the Pardoner is concerned, there is a real possibility that among his pilgrim audience there are those who might do so, and his avarice knows no close season. The mistake he makes is to call on the Host, as ruler of the pilgrimage, to kiss the relics and to insult him at the same time. His insult may be deserved, for the Host is a great swearer, but for the first time the power of the Pardoner's tongue is not enough. The Host explodes in a splendid insult in turn, which goes straight to the Pardoner's weakest spot, and the man who lives by his tongue is — the ultimate disaster — unable to reply.

The situation is very funny, of course. But behind the laughter, both of the pilgrims and ourselves, lies something rather serious. On the one hand, to laugh at the Pardoner, to see his ultimate folly, is to strip him of his power; the same has been said of his master the devil. Yet laughing at this pardoner's discomfiture does not remove his fellows from our midst, be we pilgrims on the road to Canterbury or not, for the Pardoner's modern descendants are many, and in many walks of life; the evil remains with us and is tacitly tolerated by us, and we still find it interesting, even admirable. While we may see the Pardoner ultimately subverted by the tale he tells, that tale was still told to an audience that deserved it, and genuinely needed a pardon he does not believe in.

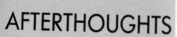

AFTERTHOUGHTS

1

What do you understand by 'black comedy' (page 47)? How appropriate is this term to *The Pardoner's Tale*?

2

Why does Moseley describe 'inner despair' as 'the deepest blasphemy' (page 48)?

3

Who do you take to be the Pardoner's 'modern descendants' (page 53)?

4

What ironies are explored in this essay?

Michael Read
*Michael Read is Senior Lecturer in
English at Paddington College and an
experienced A-level examiner.*

ESSAY

The tale outside the Tale: the Pardoner and the Host

This essay has two aims: firstly, to say something illuminating about the framing narrative of *The Pardoner's Tale*; secondly, to illustrate some of the insights offered by an approach which regards the pilgrims as realistic portraits conceived within a naturalistically depicted social world. Until relatively recently, this approach would have been taken for granted but, as a glance at the relevant volume in the *Twentieth Century Views* series makes clear, things have changed. There is an increased tendency to see the Pardoner primarily as a symbolic figure; much scholarship has been devoted to attempting to prove that a psychological approach to character is alien to medieval literature. Consequently, it is necessary at the outset to justify my approach.

    The philosopher William of Occam, who lived about half a century before his countryman Chaucer, is remembered by non-specialists, if at all, for one assertion: 'Entities are not to be multiplied without necessity.' The proposition is called Occam's razor, because it cuts away unnecessary argument. In more simple language, it means we should not invent evidence to explain a phenomenon if it can be explained on the basis of evidence already existing — an excellent principle for any form of academic study. To apply it to Chaucer's method, there is ample clear evidence that he intended his characters to be seen as 'real'. Two simple examples, neither directly concerned with *The Pardoner's Tale*, should make my point. In the last line of the portrait of the Friar, the narrator, as if in an afterthought, adds 'This worthy lymytour was cleped Huberd'. Why give him a name unless we are intended to see him as an individual rather than a type? In the next portrait, that of the Merchant, the same principle operates in reverse. The last line here is 'But, sooth to seyn, I noot how men hym calle' — 'But, to tell the truth, I didn't catch his name': just what we would say about someone rather colourless in real life.

It is important to draw the right conclusion from this kind of evidence. Because we know that at least one of the characters (Harry Bailly, landlord of the Tabard) was a real person, and because of the wealth of specific names and places cited, it is tempting to imagine we are reading a documentary account of an actual journey to Canterbury. But this is a red herring: what matters is not journalistic 'truth', but verisimilitude — the plausible *imitation* of reality. Chaucer's own presence as a character among the pilgrims is a final touch; he is inviting us to consider the fictional space the pilgrims inhabit as an area where people can be understood and judged by the same criteria as we would apply in real life, an area that mimics the real world so closely that the poet can plausibly place a fictional but recognisable portrait of himself in it.

The conflict between the Host and the Pardoner provides one of the most psychologically intense moments in the framing narrative. It derives its strength not just from the tale that precedes it, but from the power, clarity and subtlety with which both characters have already been depicted. 'Power', in fact, is a crucial issue, for both are men who derive great satisfaction from exercising their power over others, so that their confrontation can be seen as the climax of a battle for supremacy.

Harry Bailly asserts his supremacy at the start of the pilgrimage, and takes evident pleasure in exercising it as master of ceremonies and literary critic. His power springs from two sources: his outsize personality (in other words, his capacity to react and respond on a large scale), and the confidence of his judgements, whether moral, personal, or aesthetic. But though his oaths are more vivid and frequent, his scurrility more inventive, and his capacity for ridicule more hurtful, his reactions and judgements are essentially those of the ordinary man, with all the limitations that this no doubt patronising expression implies. One of the minor but significant pleasures of the framing narrative lies in observing the way the Host is outmanoeuvred by subtler minds-or more determined personalities. 'Straw for youre gentillesse!' he tells the Franklin, and receives in return a tale extolling precisely that virtue. He mocks the Clerk's study of rhetoric and we are rewarded with a tale full of the most subtle rhetorical devices. The Parson repays the accusation of Lollardry (an early form of Protestant dissent), that was provoked by his condemnation of the Host's oaths, with a lengthy and implacably serious sermon.

Yet, as these examples suggest, the Host's power can only be overcome by indirect means, not head-on conflict. I confess I find something almost alarming in this picture of banal opinions exercising such authority. For, to state the adverse case at its strongest, Harry Bailly is a bully (obsequious to his social superiors, of course) who throughout the journey to Canterbury utters not one perceptive comment on the tales. Significantly, the tale that elicits his greatest enthusiasm is that of the Nun's Priest: more significantly, his greatest praise is reserved for the Nun's Priest's burly virility:

> For if thou have corage as thou hast myght,
> Thee were nede of hennes, as I wene,
> Ya, moo than seven tymes seventene.
> See, whiche braunes hath this gentil preest,
> So gret a nekke, and swich a large breest!'

(VII, ll.3452–3456)

So it should hardly surprise us that he finds a natural enemy in the emasculated Pardoner. In a tone, elegantly described by Gabriel Josipovici[1] as 'sneering bonhomie', he invites him to tell

---

[1] G D Josipovici — 'Fiction and Game in *The Canterbury Tales*', *Critical Quarterly* VII (1965).

'som myrthe or japes' to counteract the bleak injustice of the Physician's tale. Then comes one of the most interesting moments in the framing narrative. The 'gentils' as a group rebel against this apparently reasonable suggestion — the only time the Host is challenged by a group of pilgrims. Why? Surely not because of any rooted objection to 'ribaudye': it is explicitly stated that no one except the Reeve is angered by the bawdry of the Miller's tale. Nor, as the Friar's tale shows, is there any absolute objection to bawdry from the mouth of a churchman. No, they fear the Pardoner's 'ribaudye' will strike deeper, that it will exercise a corrupting force, for they have recognised in him the other truly powerful figure in their company.

The Pardoner's supreme evil is a critical commonplace, and I have no wish to challenge this moral judgement. But moral judgements are not the only comments we can make on character. In the context of a narrative competition, it is almost as significant to point out that the Pardoner is the only conscious artist among the pilgrims (with the very ambivalent exception of Chaucer himself). That is, he prospers through his skill in oratory and narrative, and takes evident delight in the exercise and demonstration of this skill. The point can be underlined by glancing at the number of pilgrims who either apologise for their plain speaking and lack of rhetorical ability, or state at the outset that they have derived their tale from another source. None of this for the Pardoner: his prologue and tale are intended to impress his audience with his own cleverness:

> For though myself be a full vicious man,
> A moral tale yet I yow telle kan

(ll.459–460)[2]

These lines are frequently cited as indicative of the Pardoner's effrontery and of course they are, but they have a resonance that extends beyond this one tale. They are the artist's plea not to be identified with his work — a plea Chaucer himself would have endorsed heartily. He is so capable of creating and seeing

---

[2] See 'A note on the text' (p. 8) regarding line references.

through the eyes of his characters that his own identity remains elusive. The whole moral dubiousness of the fiction-writer's enterprise (pretending to be someone you are not, telling stories that are not true) is highlighted by *The Canterbury Tales*, and Chaucer's uneasy awareness is highlighted by his introduction to *The Miller's Tale*:

> The Miller is a cherl, ye knowe wel this.
> So was the Reve eek and othere mo,
> And harlotrie they tolden bothe two.
> Avyseth yow, and put me out of blame;
> And eek men shall nat maken ernest of game.
>
> (I, ll.3182–3186)

Is not the Pardoner Chaucer's *alter ego*, the evil teller of moral tales confronting, as if in a mirror, the respectable recounter of fabliaux?

No one, at any rate, could deny the Pardoner's artistry, either in the florid rhetoric of his sermon or the bleak understatement of the tale itself. Only one aspect directly concerns me here. The sermon violently and wittily attacks drunkenness and blasphemy; the tale starts in a tavern, and it is the tavern-keeper's ludicrous assertion that Death inhabits a nearby village that sets the rioters off on their quest. In passing, the Pardoner refers to tavernkeepers' practice of adulterating good-quality French wine with cheaper Spanish produce. These remarks seem clearly directed at the Host, purveyor of wine and vivid blasphemer. Even the attack on avarice may be a glance at Harry Bailly, for, whoever wins the contest, he will be the one to profit. All this suggests that the final apparently humorous attack on the Host is not an improvisation, but the true climax of the Pardoner's performance.

Consequently I question the notion of the Pardoner's 'confession':

> And lo, sires, thus I preche.
> And Jhesu Crist, that is oure soules leche,
> So graunte yow his pardoun to receyve,
> For that is best; I wol yow nat deceyve.
>
> (ll.915–918)

G L Kittredge famously describes this as 'a very paroxysm of agonised sincerity.'[3] Bertrand H Bronson[4] explains its discordance with what immediately precedes and follows it as the result of Chaucer's careless workmanship. I should like to hazard the suggestion that the lines are not a confession at all: 'And lo, sires, thus I preche' seems always to have been taken as a comment on the preceding sermon and tale; but surely it is more usual for the words 'lo' and 'thus' to refer to something about to be said or done. Could not the Pardoner be saying, in effect, 'I am so much in control of my audience that I can even admit the superior effectiveness of Christ's pardon without harming my sales'? Far from a dropping of the mask, it is a neat conclusion to his demonstration; not 'sincerity', but the ultimate effrontery.

What follows, far from being a 'wild orgy of reckless jesting' (Kittredge again) is as calculated as everything else the Pardoner says. Now at last he is directly addressing the pilgrims again, and surely we are not intended to believe that he is really trying to sell pardons. One of the qualities of a successful salesman is good judgement; another is plausibility. If the Pardoner is serious, he shows neither here: obviously he can hardly hope to sell his pardons having exposed his methods and motives; nor can he expect anyone to believe his absurd suggestion that one or *two* might break their necks on a sedate ride to Canterbury. If, however, he is joking, the exaggerations fall into place. Why should he be joking? In a general sense, to win the acceptance of his fellow-pilgrims, to present himself as a lovable rogue rather than a monster; in short, to sell *himself*: to prepare the ground for his humorous assault on the Host:

> I rede that oure Hoost heere shal bigynne,
> For he is moost envoluped in synne.
> Com forth, sire Hoost, and offre first anon,
> And thou shalte kisse the relikes everychon,
> Ye, for a grote! Unbokele anon thy purs.

(ll.941–945)

To appreciate the full subtlety of the Pardoner's performance, we

---

[3] G L Kittredge, *Chaucer and his Poetry* (Cambridge, Mass, 1915). Although I disagree with Kittredge's argument here, I recommend this book as a wonderfully accessible and enthusiastic introduction to Chaucer's work.
[4] Bertrand H Bronson, *In Search of Chaucer* (Toronto, 1960).

need to recapitulate. Invited by the Host in heavily patronising tones ('beel amy') to tell 'som myrthe or japes', but prevented by the gentils from doing so, he has revenged himself on both. He has told a moral tale in the service of corruption, revealing a frightening gap between the ability to preach morals with the utmost conviction and the desire to practise them. But he has interwoven with this an attack on the Host, a man whose coarse masculinity represents exactly what the Pardoner despises and lacks, a man whose simple attitudes and appetites make him a grotesquely inflated image of the 'lewed peple'. For in the terms of the sermon and tale, the Host, avaricious blasphemer, panderer to drunkenness and gluttony, instigator of 'hasardrye' (the lot-drawing with which the tale-contest begins) is indeed the most 'envoluped in synne'. Does the Host realise the subtlety of the web the Pardoner has spun? Of course not, but it doesn't matter; however subtle a web a spider spins, it can't entrap a bird, or, to vary the metaphor, the most skilful fencer will be defeated by the clumsiest wielder of a machine gun. It is not easy to decide whether the outburst is one of outrage or jocular insult but Harry Bailly's expression of emotion is always forceful rather than precise. What is clear is that he annihilates the Pardoner. Starting with a powerful ambiguity — '"Nay, nay!" quod he, "thanne have I Cristes curs!"', either 'May I be cursed by Christ if I kiss your relics' or 'I won't kiss your relics even if it means my being cursed by Christ' — he states the obvious with robust force:

> Thou woldest make me kisse thyn olde breech,
> And swere it were a relyk of a seint,
> Though it were with thy fundement depeint!

(ll.948–950)

Well, of course! This is exactly what the Pardoner has been telling the pilgrims; for all we know, it might be the literal truth. Yet it is a comment well designed to wound him. His sermon has revealed a disgust with human bodily functions.

> O wombe! O bely! O stynkyng cod,
> Fulfilled of dong and of corrupcioun!
> At either ende of thee foul is the soun.

(ll.534–536)

Now the host is reminding him of his own physicality. Then it is only a short journey from 'fundement' to 'coillons':

> But, by the croys which that Seint Eleyne fond,
> I wolde I hadde thy coillons in myn hond
> In stide of relikes or of seintuarie.
> Lat kutte hem of, I wol thee helpe hem carie;
> They shul be shryned in an hogges toord!

(ll.951–955)

It is a cruel irony for the Pardoner (connoisseur of irony as he is) that this spontaneous outburst hits its target so neatly. Despite the claims of some commentators, it must surely be partly an accidental hit; it would not make sense to talk about cutting off the Pardoner's testicles if the Host thought him a eunuch. So the Host's jibe is more effective even than he intends; the Pardoner's relics are worth less than a eunuch's testicles! The point of the joke is not lost upon the Pardoner — hence his angry silence. The Host's improvised eloquence (notice the brilliant casual blasphemy of 'shryned') has rendered futile the Pardoner's whole artistry. Though an outward reconciliation follows (and perhaps it is a small success for the Pardoner that the Host has to be reconciled rather than act as reconciler) — there can be no re-establishment of harmony.

So far I have treated the protagonists as individuals; now I wish to draw together some of the thematic implications of their conflict. To say characters are realistically depicted, even individualised, does not rule out the possibility of their standing as representatives of human qualities. In other words, realism can coexist with symbolism; indeed, this notion is surely at the heart of realist literature. Viewed in this light it seems clear that the Pardoner stands for the artist, the Host for his audience. The very structure of *The Canterbury Tales* draws the reader's attention to the fact that stories are 'made'; they are artifices, not slices of life, however much they may resemble it. I have already suggested that, in his portrayal of the Pardoner, Chaucer confronts the moral ambiguities of his own profession. It then follows that in depicting Harry Bailly, he is venting his frustrations at his unresponsive or inappropriately responsive audience.

Every reader who loves Chaucer must wonder why he speaks so directly to us over six centuries. *The Pardoner's*

Prologue and Tale raises the question with particular force: why should we be interested in the exposition of the tricks of a strange and obsolete trade, or a sermon expounding beliefs we can no longer share or have much sympathy with? Partly, of course, because forceful and inventive writing is always of interest. But it is not just this: as long as we read or listen to stories, and maybe invent them ourselves, we will be fascinated by works that question the whole enterprise. The duel between impotent word-spinner and virile philistine should disturb all who believe in the power of words.

A final point adds weight to this argument. Something that puzzles many readers is that the conventionally pious Host should blaspheme so enthusiastically, at one point attracting the adverse comment of the Parson for so doing. Viewed in this context, the reason is obvious; blasphemies are mere words, and so he finds no contradiction between his faith and his actions, for words are not actions. The Pardoner can only act through words and thus falls victim to a crowning irony; he is defeated, in words, by someone who rejects their power. But Chaucer's irony encloses Pardoner, Host and reader: the Pardoner because this master of words is silenced by coarse buffoonery; the Host because, in the very act of silencing his adversary, he proves the power of the words he rejects; and the reader because, once we have registered the ironies, the questioning of fiction and of language itself, we still cannot dispel from our minds the images Chaucer has created: an old man directing drunken thugs down the crooked path to death; a lank-haired eunuch and a tavern-keeper engaged in a battle of wills, somewhere between Southwark and Canterbury.

AFTERTHOUGHTS

1

Compare Read's view of Chaucer's approach to characterisation
with the views expressed by Spencer Ellis in his essay (pages
29–44). Do you agree that Chaucer intended his characters to be
seen as 'real' (page 56)?

2

What reasons does Read give for suggesting that the Pardoner
might be 'Chaucer's *alter ego*' (page 59)?

3

Do you agree that the Host is the most 'envoluped in synne' of
the pilgrims (page 61)?

4

What parallels are drawn in this essay between the relationship
between the Pardoner and the Host and the relationship between an artist and his audience?

Paul Oliver

Paul Oliver is a member of the English Department and Director of Drama at Forest School.

ESSAY

Confusion and concealment in *The Pardoner's Tale*

Readers of *The Pardoner's Tale* tend to interpret it along one of two lines. It's seen as meaning either that those who love money will die or that an addiction to money leads one to commit other sins as well. But do these interpretations really make sense of the tale? If the Pardoner is bluntly asserting that those who are avaricious can expect to die, it's tempting to speculate what will happen to everyone else. And if the avaricious do die in their sinful state more or less automatically (and presumably go to hell just as automatically, though there's no mention of that in the tale), there would be little point in paying the Pardoner for one of his pardons or for being allowed to kiss his relics. No doubt it is possible in theory to take the physical death of the three men in the tale as an allegory of their spiritual death, but this isn't really satisfactory: in lines 547–548,[1] 'But, certes, he that haunteth swiche delices/ Is deed, whil that he lyveth in tho

---

[1] See 'A note on the text' (p.8) regarding line references.

vices,' the Pardoner is very clear that it's feasible to be clinically alive while spiritually dead — so a tale that showed *physical* death to be the result of avarice would run the risk of badly clouding the issue.

If we take the other, perhaps more popular overall interpretation and see in the men's mutual murder one effect of living an avaricious life, the force of the story as a whole is, it seems to me, sadly weakened: we know from our experience of life outside the tale that most people, even most avaricious people, do not commit murder. In any case, the climax is not a watertight illustration of the notion that love of money does lead to murder and death: one of the two older men, perhaps even both of them, could presumably have drunk from the uncontaminated bottle and survived, at least for the time being. The apparent moral, whichever of the two you take it to be (and the difference is only really a question of emphasis according to whether you see the men as each other's murderers or each other's victims), is contradicted anyway by the Pardoner himself who, on his own admission, is deeply avaricious — there is hardly anything else to his character — but who prospers remarkably. (See, for example, lines 703–706 of the *General Prologue* for evidence of his conspicuous success from outside his own performance.)

This basic problem of meaning has two main. causes, one external to the Pardoner and one very much bound up with his character. The first is that the style of *The Pardoner's Tale*, with its exclamations, repetitions and lurid vividness, and also the subject matter and structure are all shaped by its being designed for oral performance in church. A carefully worked out logic is not necessarily an important ingredient of the classic sermon: the preacher narrating a story needs a plot that is fast-moving, makes a powerful impression and in some way draws in or implicates his audience. If these requirements are fulfilled, then those listening will readily cooperate with the speaker and the context in the production of meaning. Applying these criteria to *The Pardoner's Tale*, we may note that the Pardoner implies to his pilgrim-hearers that they are going to witness an illustration of his habitual theme, '*Radix malorum est Cupiditas*' (ll.334 and 426). To the men's several vices mentioned in the opening lines of the tale proper, and inveighed against by the Pardoner, is eventually added avarice, which appears to lead to their deaths. We oblige the narrator and supply one of the two 'meanings' I began by outlining. But what's really happened is that we've become caught up in the oral performance and have assumed that because the Pardoner said that his theme is always '*Radix malorum est Cupiditas*', it must therefore be so here — and we have taken a hint from the men's discovery of gold/death under the tree. Interestingly, when the narrative finishes, the Pardoner draws attention to something of overwhelming triviality, the symptoms of poisoning exhibited by the dead men, and then returns to inveighing against all the vices except, as it happens, avarice! It's true that he established the interconnectedness of the various vices earlier, but still noticeable that avarice is not mentioned again until he turns to his imaginary church audience in order to urge them to shun it (1.905). But so keen are we to supply meanings, so trained from our earliest experience of having things read to us to see patterns, that we are more than willing to cooperate in clearing up the general confusion.

The second reason for the tale's lack of strict logic is the Pardoner's own spiritual blindness, which is bound to cause his handling of any vaguely spiritual matter to be done in vivid poster-paint colours. Being oblivious to all spiritual considerations, the Pardoner is hardly in a position to point out the same state in others. Although his hypocrisy in many areas is such that we know he would not hesitate on that account (he is proud, after all, of attacking the vice he practises), he is entirely lacking in the necessary perception. If he possessed it once, he has since ruthlessly suppressed it in the interests of making money. The reference to spiritual death in lines 547–548 has a coldly theoretical ring: the lines are essentially part of the Pardoner's patter and are delivered in the same mechanical way as, for instance, his biblical examples. In our enthusiastic haste to interpret (over-interpret?) the tale, we credit the three men with spiritual blindness. But this is not what the Pardoner sees in them: he sees merely the practice of vice or rather, specific vices (as the denunciations following the men's deaths show), not the spiritual condition which links the practice of the vices or its effects in eschatological terms. Notice that the Pardoner does not say that the men's souls went to hell (as we would expect) or even that they would have spent less time in purgatory had they insured themselves against a lengthy stay there by a sensible outlay on pardons like those carried by the Pardoner. His interest in the three men ends with their deaths. Paradoxically (in view of how he makes a living), he is not concerned about the fate of people's souls. But then, how could he be, without being forced to consider his own spiritual state? Even when he wishes to impress on his hearers a sense of the terrifying fragility of human existence and their good fortune in having a spiritual first-aid man travelling with them, he talks about the moment 'Whan that the soule shal fro the body passe' (1.940): the moment of death, without reference to the soul's destination. It's not a polite euphemism to avoid the thought of death: it's a form of words designed to avoid looking beyond.

He does use a euphemism — once — when referring to the souls of his 'victims': 'I rekke nevere, whan that they been beryed,/ Though that hir soules goon a-blakeberyed' (ll.405–406). The contempt behind the lines takes attention away from the euphemistic nature of the phrase, but it's typical of the Pardoner's habits of thought and speech to represent the after-life of the damned in everyday, earthbound terms. He does, it's true, say to those about to make offerings to him, 'Into the blisse of hevene shul ye gon' (1.912), but, significantly, this envisages the after-life of the *saved* and is, in any case, part of the memorised and mechanically delivered sample sermon, at one remove from the direct and riskier discourse with his pilgrim-audience which contains the remark about the soul leaving the body. (Whether or not the Pardoner coined the blackberrying euphemism, one can't help noticing that in avoiding a direct remark about hell, he uses more vivid language than when directly mentioning its opposite: 'entering the bliss of heaven' must have been a preacher's cliché long before the Pardoner used it.)

This refusal to contemplate the other-worldly in any but the most superficial way is on a par with the Pardoner's denial of possibly beneficial side-effects to his work. So that there shall be no doubt at all about his motives, he declares:

> Of avarice and of swich cursednesse
> Is all my prechyng, for to make hem free
> To yeven hir pens, and namely unto me.
> For myn entente is nat but for to wynne,

And nothyng for correccioun of synne.

(ll.400–404)

This amazing self-condemnation is a proud boast, but in the end it can only serve to undermine the Pardoner's authority and that of his performance.

The sense that *The Pardoner's Tale* contains depths hidden from its narrator or into which he refuses to look is particularly strong when the three revellers speak to the old man before leaving him behind in their headlong rush to find Death. From this point of view it's convenient that the men forget him instantly. We do not. And yet, far from indicating how this curiously evocative (and controversial) figure should be interpreted, the Pardoner seems almost unaware of his presence in his narrative. I want to suggest that the old man seriously threatens to disturb the Pardoner's self-satisfaction and peace of mind and therefore, in a sense, *has* to be ignored. For however much the Pardoner wishes to appear a moral authority with his Latin tags and scriptural examples, he can never be more than a bogus authority. His attitude to his material is purely exploitative. He puts it colourfully, but the truth is clear: 'in Latyn I speke a wordes fewe,/ To saffron with my predicacioun' (ll.344–345). He is hardly more of a true scholar than the three revellers in his narrative. The old man, on the other hand, is a very real moral authority. He means what he says; he can tie in scriptural references with his own experience; above all, he steals a march on the men by taking over the moral and dramatic initiative at this point in the tale. Although the men's wickedness prevents them ever really having the moral upper hand, their crusade-like quest for Death on behalf of their stricken acquaintance has made them feel self-righteous. As for the dramatic initiative, until now the men have *acted*. When they meet the old man, they are forced to listen to a thirty-line discourse on old age and how it should be respected, which temporarily silences even their rudeness.

If the tale threatens to disturb its own equilibrium by developing the old man independently of the needs of the plot and by placing at its centre the figure of an altruistic preacher, it's perhaps as well to be clear about what useful function he performs. To argue that his inclusion is accounted for by the presence in the source material of a similar figure won't do, since we know that Chaucer was ordinarily quite happy to manipulate his sources for his own artistic ends, adding, omitting, changing emphases and so on. Perhaps something of the rationale behind his use of the old man can be seen if we imagine *The Pardoner's Tale* without him: three men hear of the death of a friend; they set out to kill Death, with revenge as their motive; their search happens to be successful; they kill one another. It's obvious what is missing: a richness — a sense that it all means something more than the obvious and crudely superficial. Think, for instance, of the warning contained in the old man's 'if that ye so longe abyde' (l.747) or his wonderfully suggestive 'if that yow be so leef/ To fynde Deeth, turne up this croked wey' (ll.760–761), which makes the landscape suddenly become menacingly symbolic as the domesticity of the original tavern setting recedes into the background. The men's loss of the dramatic initiative is important because it serves as a reminder that they are not as free as they would like to think they are. No doubt technically they could abandon their love of material things (and their search for Death) even at this point, but with evil and lack of moral awareness both set in so deeply, we know that it's unlikely that there will be any change. The narrator says later that the devil was allowed to tempt the youngest man to buy poison 'For-why the feend foond hym in swich lyvyng/ That he hadde leve him to sorwe bryng' (ll.847–848). Those bent on damning themselves don't actually need much assistance from external sources. In one respect the old man, who is not his own agent and is moved by a strange compulsion to act as he does, presents the three men with a distorted image of themselves. In other ways (by his constant tramping of the earth and knocking on it) he remains a mystery which stubbornly refuses to be neatly woven into the main thread of the narrative.

Another potentially disruptive element in *The Pardoner's Tale* is the biblical and related references which are generally taken to function as 'acted-out' blasphemies. The revellers, for example, are seen as usurping Christ's function as conqueror of death: 'Deeth shal be deed, if that they may hym hente' (l.710). Readers with an ear for this sort of echo have detected in the conspiracy of the senior two to kill the youngest (significantly, by stabbing him in the side in the manner of Christ on the cross) a reference to a medieval heresy: the idea that Christ was not after all a willing sufferer but the victim of a conspiracy on the part of God the Father and the Holy Spirit. They have seen in the celebratory drinking of wine over the corpse of the youngest man a hint of the Last Supper. But it's important to understand what these blasphemous parodies achieve, beyond gratifying the erudite reader. They're usually seen as blackening the men still further. But *is* it the revellers who are incriminated by these blasphemies? Isn't it actually the Pardoner, marshalling and structuring the material, who is committing them? The three men are, in line with one's expectations, supremely ignorant of their Christ-usurping role: it is the Pardoner who helps to impose this on them by his form of words: the use of a kind of reported speech in line 710 does not suggest for a moment that the men think of themselves as Christ-style death-killers. Similarly, we're made aware of the likeness of this unholy trio to the Holy Trinity by constant reminders of their relative ages: 'And it fil on the yongeste of hem alle' (l.804); 'This yongeste, which that wente to the toun' (l.837); and so on. In a shockingly literal way the two older men drink damnation to themselves at the end. There's surely a reference here to 1 Corinthians 11, verse 29: 'he who eats and drinks unworthily eats and drinks his own judgement if he does not discern the body of the Lord'. (My translation from the Vulgate, the only version of the Bible easily available to Chaucer.) If it is the Pardoner who is guilty of blasphemy by, as it were, working it into the structure of his tale, then the tale incriminates its narrator as deeply as its protagonists — if not far more, seeing that the Pardoner has set himself up as authority and judge. Indeed, the more you consider it, the more similarities emerge between the Pardoner and the three men: all four are spiritually dead; they are blasphemers and motivated by avarice; all are so carried away by the momentum of their life-styles that, in spite of the theoretical possibility of repentance already mentioned, they are in practical terms totally hardened sinners. If we shared the religious assumptions of the text's original audience, we would be forced to conclude that the Pardoner's indifference to the spiritual welfare of his hearers is the strongest possible proof that he 'Is deed, whil that he lyveth in tho vices' (l.548): with each recital of his story, the Pardoner figuratively drinks judgement to himself.

Should we see the Pardoner as aware of the blasphemies he commits? This is a very dangerous line of enquiry and reminiscent of the attempt to psychoanalyse Hamlet. It implies an autonomous existence for the Pardoner when he is really as much at the mercy of Chaucer's creative processes as the three revellers themselves. It was Chaucer's peculiar genius to construct brilliantly lively narrators for stories whose basic materials were largely traditional: the *persona* of the Pardoner and the illusion of performance given by *The Pardoner's Prologue and Tale* are much greater testimonies to the poet's inventiveness than the tale of the search for Death. Treating the Pardoner as a character in the novelistic sense is merely a critical convenience which allows us to examine aspects of the performance assigned to him. But if we refuse to entertain the illusion of the independent existence of the narrators of *The Canterbury Tales*, we miss rich veins both of comic irony and sharp-edged satire embedded in the text. So many of *The Canterbury Tales* work — or are made to work — against their narrator. The Knight, for example, tells a tale which shows up the limitations and absurdities of the chivalric code he professes to follow; the narrators of the two tales which follow his, the Miller and the Reeve, tell stories in which working men like themselves are outwitted by men of learning. Therefore, if we see the Pardoner as unaware of his own blasphemies (as we would expect from one as spiritually blind and inept as the actors in his drama), he becomes a victim of the same process. In any case, to face up to the blasphemies in his tale would be the same as for the Pardoner to confront the thought of life after death. It would force him to be aware of spiritual values on whose suppression his success depends. Like the Friar described in the *General Prologue*, the Pardoner cashes in on people's fears for their well-being in the after-life, but puts the emphasis entirely on the financial process which allegedly guarantees this well-being:

> Myn hooly pardoun may yow alle warice,
> So that ye offre nobles or sterlynges,
> Or elles silver broches, spoones, rynges.

(ll.906–908)

The power of *The Pardoner's Tale* in spite of its lack of strict logic, its strange irrelevancies and unsolved problems is a tribute to Chaucer's sense of what entertains, moves and disturbs. To see these flaws in it is not to reduce the tale but to realise that the tale is just as much an oral performance as its prologue, and just as much a piece of self-exposure. The difference between them is that whereas in the prologue the Pardoner is proud of being confessional, in the tale he is unaware of it.

AFTERTHOUGHTS

1

Do you agree that the Pardoner has 'hardly anything else to his character' beyond being avaricious (page 66)?

2

To what extent do *you* see *'Radix malorum est Cupiditas'* as the moral of *The Pardoner's Tale*?

3

What explanation does Oliver offer for the lack of specific reference to damnation in *The Pardoner's Tale* (pages 67–69)?

4

Do you agree that *The Pardoner's Tale* 'entertains, moves and disturbs' (page 73)?

Angus Alton

Angus Alton works as a researcher for the University of Oxford Delegacy of Local Examinations. He is also an experienced examiner in English Literature at GCSE and A level.

ESSAY

The true morality of *The Pardoner's Tale*

The meaning of almost any piece of writing is heavily dependent on the context in which it is seen. And, for a variety of reasons, context is probably a more important concept for our understanding of Chaucer than it is with any other major author in English. The first of these reasons is that the period in which Chaucer wrote is more remote from us than that of any of the other most commonly studied authors. I will return to this issue later, but for the moment wish to focus on another important problem of context that he poses. It is essentially the fact that the most that you are likely to study of Chaucer's at A level is a fragment of a complete work; or rather, a fragment of a work that was never even completed. It is vital, therefore, to make use of as much information as possible that is available about the context of each individual tale, in order to inform our understanding.

This is nowhere truer than it is for *The Pardoner's Tale*, but, fortunately, this is a tale where we have abundant information available as we seek to make the fullest sense of it. At the simplest level, we are offered a brief summary of the nature of the tale as it is conceived by its teller. He tells his fellow-pilgrims:

For though myself be a ful vicious man,
A moral tale yet I yow telle kan,
Which I am wont to preche for to wynne.

(ll.459–461)[1]

This is, then, to be an example of the sort of sermon that the
Pardoner regularly preaches, and it is in response to a request
for 'som moral thyng' (l.325) from his fellow-pilgrims. We even
have a clear idea of what is to be the 'sentence' of the sermon,
for:

My theme is alwey oon, and evere was —
Radix malorum est Cupiditas.

(ll.333–334)

Given all this, the title of this essay may seem a little suprising,
unless, that is, the tale were not an illustration of the moral
already outlined. But of course it *is* a powerful warning of the
dangers of covetousness: no one, surely, could miss the point of
the need to 'ware yow fro the synne of avarice' (l.905). What is
more, the subsidiary morals of the tale are just as explicit, just
as effectively made:

And now that I have spoken of glotonye,
Now wol I yow deffenden hasardrye.

(ll.589–590)

In short, the tale is a specimen of how the Pardoner seeks, as he
puts it in the quotation above, to 'wynne', and as such it should
be no surprise that the morals in it are clear, indeed, clearly
stated. But my point would be that what we have looked at so
far is the morality of the Pardoner's *tale*; what I wish to try and
tease out is the true morality of *The Pardoner's Tale*. That is,
why does Chaucer give this tale to the Pardoner, and what does
that reveal about the overall impact of *The Canterbury Tales*? In
other words, we are into the ever-important area of the relationship of the teller to the tale, and here, of course, context is
highly relevant.

When considering *The Pardoner's Tale*, we have several

---

[1] See 'A note on the text' (p. 8) regarding line references.

sources of information for that context. First, we have, as we do when considering most of the other tales, a description of the man in the *General Prologue*. This description, like most others, is rich with implications and irony, so that we learn quite as much about the personality of the Pardoner as we do about his appearance. In addition to this source, we also have, as we do for at least several of the tales, much of the context into which the tale was to be set. We know, for example, which tale precedes it in the overall structure of the poem: *The Physician's Tale*; we know, too, how the two tales were going to be linked; and we know how the tale is received by the pilgrims. There is also one further source of information about the Pardoner and his tale, and it is a source shared with only one of the other pilgrims that we know about: both the Pardoner and the Wife of Bath are given substantial prologues of their own. These serve as kinds of personal statements, and thus allow us much more direct insight into the personalities concerned. They also, incidentally, provide some kind of answer to a nagging question which underlies any reading of the *General Prologue*: how does Chaucer, the pilgrim who is with the others on the way to Canterbury, know the background information about his fellow-pilgrims?

In this context, there is a slight oddity in what is normally said about these two pilgrims in particular. They are, we are confidently informed, hypocrites. It is, of course, easy to see why they should be considered hypocritical, and, indeed, in some sense it is a fair accusation. But it must be acknowledged as a very special kind of hypocrisy. For a start, there is no hint in the Pardoner, as there often is with hypocrites, of self-deception:

> Thus kan I preche agayn that same vice
> Which that I use, and that is avarice.

                                                                    (ll.427–428)

There is no attempt here, as there is with the wealthy American evangelists, to quieten conscience by claiming that everything is done for the greater glory of the Lord. It should be remembered how easy an excuse that would be to develop for someone engaged in the Pardoner's line of work. Even more unusually for hypocrites, there seems to be little real attempt by the Pardoner, at least during the pilgrimage, to conceal his dishonesty. He cheerfully admits that he will accept gifts:

Al were it yeven of the povereste page,
Or of the povereste wydwe in a village,
Al sholde hir children sterve for famyne.

(ll.449–451)

And perhaps most chillingly, he rather gleefully admits his own deviousness:

Thus quyte I folk that doon us displesances;
Thus spitte I out my venym under hewe
Of hoolynesse, to semen hooly and trewe.

(ll.420–422)

For the Pardoner and the Wife of Bath in particular, then, some attempt to evaluate the tale in terms of its teller seems required. In the case of the Pardoner, the fact that his tale is to follow the Physician's makes it even more important. For the reader or listener is likely to come to the Pardoner's contribution to the tale-telling competition in a rather puzzled frame of mind. The Physician, of whom we are told 'His studie was but litel on the Bible (*General Prologue*, I, l.438), has told a highly moral tale, concluding by advising:

Therfore I rede yow this conseil take:
Forsaketh synne, er synne yow forsake.

(VI, ll.285–286)

The words could easily have been spoken by the Pardoner — or the Parson. The readers begin to wonder how well they have understood the hidden messages of the *General Prologue*, or perhaps to doubt the accuracy of the information it supplies.

It is thus with some relief when the Host turns to the Pardoner for 'som myrthe or japes' (l.319) that almost everything that follows serves to confirm the view we form of the man during the *General Prologue*. His first action is to have a drink of 'corny ale' (l.315), and he virtually admits that his relics are false:

Relikes been they, as wenen they echoon

(l.349)

going on to describe his whole strategy as a 'gaude' (l.389). Even the claim to 'have a joly wenche in every toun' (l.453) is sufficiently in keeping with the general air of vice that surrounds the Pardoner in the *General Prologue* even if it is not quite consonant with some of the implications of his description. Indeed, the connections are so clear that it is easy to regard *The Pardoner's Prologue and Tale* as straightforward reflections of the character as introduced in the *General Prologue*. The man's greed, dishonesty and avarice are transparently clear in all we learn of him, and the complete absence of any religious scruples is in abundant evidence in his prologue. His 'entente' he tells us is 'nothyng for correccioun of synne' (ll.403–404).

But these connections are by no means the whole story. For a start, there is one aspect of the Pardoner's character which, while it is frequently suggested to us, it is all too easy to overlook as we rail against his vices. He is a very successful preacher. The *General Prologue* tells us that he 'ful wel koude' 'affile his tonge/ To wynne silver' (I, ll.712–713) and he puts a figure on his success in his own prologue: 'An hundred mark' (1.390). He even provides a marvellous glimpse of himself at work:

> Thanne peyne I me to strecche forth the nekke,
> And est and west upon the peple I bekke,
> As dooth a dowve sittynge on a berne.
> Myne handes and my tonge goon so yerne
> That it is joye to se my bisynesse.
>
> (ll.395–399)

In addition, it is easy to believe that he has so bewitched his audience on the pilgrimage that what was intended just as an example of how he tricks money out of 'lewed peple' (1.392) has almost become an opportunity for further gain. We can imagine a moment of stunned silence as the Pardoner finishes his tale, and the Pardoner tries to take advantage of this:

> But, sires, o word forgat I in my tale
>
> (1.919)

Besides, even if this is rejected as too fanciful, and without internal evidence to back it up, our own judgement of the tale must confirm how successful it is as a piece of preaching. The tale never loses sight of its central moral points; the basic story is entirely apt for those points; and the mysterious figure of the old man waiting for 'an heyre clowt to wrappe me' (l.736) creates enough uncertainty to become a talking point and thus to make the teaching memorable. It is worth noting at this point that the Pardoner's voice, 'as smal as hath a goot' (*General Prologue*, I, l.688), may have certain implications about the sexual character of the man, but it assuredly is a necessary part of his armoury as an effective preacher. Developing a sing-song and slightly high-pitched voice was a part of clerical training until comparatively recently.

But while it may be easy enough to agree on the Pardoner's abilities as a story-teller, that agreement leads on to certain implications which are not always thought through. In particular, it means that the Pardoner *does* save souls, and in large numbers. This is implicit in two of the points the Pardoner himself makes in his prologue. First he points out the irony that:

> For certes, many a predicacioun
> Comth ofte tyme of yvel entencioun

(ll.407–408)

And later he admits that:

> Yet kan I maken oother folk to twynne
> From avarice and soore to repente.

(ll.430–431)

We can, though, only be sure of this if we can be sure of how the medieval Church would have regarded repentance that was excited by an insincere speaker, and, what is more, which would have been expressed by the purchase of a — probably — forged pardon or by touching false relics. That is, the issue is again one of context: it seems to me that our final view of the Pardoner is vitally dependent on our knowing what happens — spiritually — to those 'lewed peple' he deceives.

On this point, we can rest comforted. In theological terms, the only criterion for salvation is the sincerity of the penitent. The possession of pardons, real or forged, would be irrelevant, for God sees into our heart, and thus knows the state of mind in which a pardon was purchased. This may, of course, make the whole system of pardons seem even more contemptible to our modern sensibilities, but it does let the Pardoner off the hook.

There can surely be no doubting the sincerity of that 'povereste page' and 'povereste wydwe' (ll.449, 450) when they are charitable to the Pardoner. These people's souls will not 'goon a-blakeberyed' (1.406), despite the Pardoner's lack of concern.

But, if the Pardoner can wriggle free from the hook of our anger at his deceitfulness, there is another far deeper hook on which he is impaled. It is nothing to do with our attitude; indeed, if anything it serves to soften our condemnation still further, for it elevates him to something approaching tragic status. The fact of the matter is that one soul at least is lost as a result of the Pardoner's fraudulent activities: his own. In the end, the joke will be on him.

For, like many people who are blessed with an especial talent, the Pardoner is an over-reacher. He is so filled with his own success that he doesn't notice when it leads him to disaster. Presumably, it is this self-defeating vanity that is hinted at in the account of his clothing in the *General Prologue*:

> But hood, for jolitee, wered he noon,
> For it was trussed up in his walet.
> Hym thoughte he rood al of the newe jet;
> Dischevelee, save his cappe, he rood al bare.

(I, ll.680–683)

For all that this style achieves is to reveal that his hair hangs in rats' tails. We get a further glimpse of that vanity in the passage in the Pardoner's prologue quoted earlier (ll. 395–399) when he takes pleasure in his own techniques. There is something slightly intoxicated here, and, of course, that may quite literally be the case. Early in the tale, the Pardoner uses Lot as an exemplum, warning about drunkenness:

> So dronke he was, he nyste what he wroghte

(1.487)

and it may be that the 'draughte of corny ale' (1.456) which he has himself consumed has damaged his judgement. There is an old notion that *in vino veritas* (truth is revealed by alcohol), and the Pardoner's open account of his own methods may quite simply be an example of the lowering of defences which alcohol often induces. (It should be noted, too, that the pilgrimage itself may contribute to the confessional atmosphere, even in characters as irreligious as the Pardoner: certainly it seems to lead the Merchant — who we are told in the *General Prologue* speaks only of his profits — to bemoan his disastrous marriage.)

Such speculations are, however, largely unnecessary when discussing the Pardoner. The boasting about his methods and their success is all of a piece with the over-reaching vanity which undermines him. It reaches its climax, of course, at the end of the tale. One must presume that when he starts speaking, the Pardoner really is intending to do no more than to offer an example of the kind of 'moral tale' which he is 'wont to preche for to wynne' (ll.460–461). He probably sees the opportunity to brag about his exploits as the chief source of pleasure on the pilgrimage; that and a fair chance of winning the 'soper at oure aller cost' (*General Prologue*, I, l.799) that is the prize in the story-telling competition. No doubt, by the end, he wishes that that had remained the summit of his ambitions. But so effective does he seem to have been that he simply cannot resist: he cannot turn down the possibility of some easy money. Not only that, but he chooses the Host as his first target. One is reminded of the vengeful streak that he reveals in his prologue:

> Thus quyte I folk that doon us displesances

(l.420)

and the possibility of bad blood between the Host and the Pardoner is raised. The over-reacher, though, has taken on a formidable opponent, and inevitably comes off second best. For the Host, with unerring instinct, finds the Pardoner's most vulnerable spot:

> I wolde I hadde thy coillons in myn hond
> In stide of relikes or of seintuarie.
> Lat kutte hem of, I wol thee helpe hem carie

(ll. 952–954)

Infuriated but humiliated by the precision of the Host's attack, the Pardoner is left literally speechless. The man who takes such delight in the way his tongue goes 'so yerne' (l.398) has nothing to say, and only the authority of the Knight is capable of enforcing some sort of reconciliation between the pair.

I earlier suggested that the Pardoner acquired an almost tragic status, but in the end he is never really a focus for sympathy. We delight in his humiliation, and there is no real call for any reservations about that response. But I would argue that our final response to *The Pardoner's Tale* does need to be a good deal more careful than our attitude to its teller might suggest. For a start, it is as well to remember that our knowledge of the Pardoner depends to a great extent on privileged information. The account in the *General Prologue* may be based largely on surface appearances, and thus available to all, but here too context is important. We read about the Pardoner — who, note, is the last of the pilgrims to be described — with minds alerted to Chaucer's ironic method; we are looking for all the implications. In other circumstances, the Pardoner's status and his bewitching rhetoric may make it a good deal harder to see the viciousness underneath. At the very least, then, we should learn the need to pay close attention to details.

The final equation is, in fact, a good deal more complex than that. His success as a preacher is a vital factor here. If it would be easy, in less helpful circumstances, to fail to see the Pardoner's faults, it is just as easy when they are brought clearly to our attention to forget about his talents. At one level, Chaucer seems to be warning us to know our enemies: it is foolish to underrate them. But on another level, he seems almost to be questioning whether the Pardoner *is* an enemy. Whatever his intentions may be, he is doing God's work remarkably successfully. Indeed, it is hard to resist the conclusion that he is much more likely to save souls by his preaching than the pious Parson is with his.

In this way, Chaucer has created a marvellously rich set of responses. At the simplest level is the teaching in the tale. There can be little doubt that we must accept that set of morals, partly because they are conveyed with such authority by the Pardoner. But the context in which the tale is set adds a dimension to that morality, for the Pardoner, who seems in his prologue to be well aware of his own faults, is in the end undone by precisely the greed that he preaches against, and which he acknowledges in himself. And, so long as we don't lose sight of the potential for inspiring others to goodness in the Pardoner, Chaucer allows us to be reassured that the Pardoner will gain nothing from his exploitativeness. We end our reading of *The Pardoner's Prologue and Tale*, as we began it, laughing at the

Pardoner. But, where our original laughter was largely derision of his effeminate nature and pretensions, the final joke at his expense is both finer and, perhaps, sadder: the self-confessed 'ful vicious man' is a powerful agent for good.

AFTERTHOUGHTS

1

Explain the significance of the title of this essay.

2

What is 'special' (page 77) about the Pardoner's hypocrisy?

3

Do you agree that the Pardoner 'is much more likely to save souls by his preaching than the pious Parson is with his' (page 83)?

4

In the light of the final paragraph of this essay, do you feel any sympathy for the Pardoner?

Alan Gardiner

Alan Gardiner is Lecturer in English Language and Literature at Redbridge Technical College, and is the author of numerous critical studies.

ESSAY

The Pardoner as preacher

The preaching of Chaucer's Pardoner in his prologue and tale rightly strikes most readers as a performance of extraordinary power and skill. Nevertheless, while the Pardoner is a character of memorable individuality, whose presence it is impossible to forget as we read his tale, he is at the same time a representative figure, whose preaching draws extensively on medieval conventions and traditions. Research has established that the many corrupt practices of the Pardoner were common among the pardoners (or quaestors) of fourteenth-century England. The profession had fallen into extreme disrepute and the abuses of which the Pardoner is guilty were typical: the use of forged documents to establish his authority, the exploitation of that authority for personal profit, the peddling of fake relics. Lay quaestors also frequently claimed powers of absolution — which in reality belonged only to priests — and preached from the parish pulpit, a religious function that similarly could only be performed by priests. That Chaucer's Pardoner only had lay status is indicated by his untonsured hair (described in the *General Prologue* portrait); that he nevertheless preached is shown by virtually the whole of *The Pardoner's Tale*. More specifically, he begins his prologue by describing his manner of speech 'in chirches whan I preche' (l.329)[1] and soon afterwards tells his fellow-pilgrims, 'I stonde lyk a clerk in my pulpet' (l.391).

The content of the Pardoner's preaching and the ways in which this content is organised and delivered also correspond in many respects to established medieval practice. Medieval sermons, as the principal means of dispensing religious teaching (in addition to being an important source of popular entertainment), were a highly developed art. Numerous conventions existed, and preaching manuals offered detailed guidance on structure and technique. The traditional sermon had six parts: (1) the statement of the theme, which was usually a biblical text; (2) the protheme, a kind of introduction; (3) the dilatatio, a detailed explanation of the text; (4) the exemplum, a story to illustrate the text; (5) the peroration, a discussion of the application of the text; (6) the closing formula — a final blessing. The more specific techniques recommended in the manuals included the methodical progression from point to point and the extensive use of *ensamples*. These were examples used to illustrate an argument, and could take various forms: reference to scriptural or other authorities, quotations from other writers, stories or anecdotes taken from history or from everyday experience. Also encouraged were stylistic devices such as repetition (to add emphasis and to ensure that the most important parts of the sermon were remembered), onomatopoeia and *exclamatio* (exclamatory invocations). The ultimate religious purpose of sermons was also clearly defined. The preacher received his inspiration from God and was an agent of the Holy Spirit. His preaching must therefore be in praise of God and must contain no element of vanity, no glorying in his own authority and oratorical power.

The Pardoner's preaching is clearly at odds with the last of these stipulations. He has an obvious delight in his own powers of persuasion and the purpose of his preaching, as he openly admits in his prologue, 'is nat but for to wynne,/ And nothyng for correccioun of synne' (ll.403–404). The structure of the prologue and tale, however, adheres closely albeit not completely to medieval convention. In the prologue the Pardoner is not preach-

---

[1] See 'A note on the text' (p. 8) regarding line references.

ing as such but rather describing his technique and explaining his motives to the Canterbury pilgrims. Nevertheless, the prologue does reveal that his preaching always has a theme, and that this theme is always the same biblical text — 'Radix malorum est Cupiditas'. The tale that follows is offered as an example of his preaching, and the story of the rioters that he tells is clearly the exemplum that illustrates his text. In addition, the discourse on the sins that occurs early in the tale (ll.483– 659) might be considered the dilatatio, or exposition on the text, and the series of exclamations that follow the story of the rioters (ll.904–915), the peroration. Finally, there is a closing benediction, although this occurs when the Pardoner has concluded the demonstration of his preaching and is again directly addressing the pilgrims (ll.916–918). In the course of his preaching, the Pardoner also relies heavily on the stylistic techniques associated with medieval sermons: there is much use of repetition, exclamation and other rhetorical devices, and his arguments, especially in the discourse on the sins, are copiously supported by *ensamples* from a variety of sources.

What makes most impression on us, of course, is not the presence of these conventions but the skill with which they are applied. The energy and emotional force of the Pardoner's preaching are irresistible: the stylistic devices mentioned above and the shifts in tone required by the conventional sermon structure are exploited to their fullest effect. This means that as a sermon against avarice the Pardoner's tale is very effective, creating a genuine fear of sin — as the Pardoner himself recognises:

> Yet kan I maken oother folk to twynne
> From avarice, and soore to repente.

(ll.430–431)

The Pardoner also points out the irony in this — that the sin of which he is himself most guilty is the one that he preaches against. By making people ashamed of their avarice he encourages them to part with their money and so feeds his own greed — the true motive behind the Pardoner's passionate denunciations of sinfulness. The Pardoner's intimate knowledge of the world of sin he ostensibly condemns also gives his preaching a quality of vivid realism it would not otherwise have — in his attacks upon gluttony, drunkenness and blasphemy, we sense that the Pardoner is able to evoke the reality of these sins so convincingly because he is drawing on his own experience of them.

In the description of his preaching technique that the Pardoner gives in his prologue (as a prelude to the extended demonstration of that technique in the tale), he emerges as a shrewd and self-conscious manipulator, able to stand back from his own performance in the pulpit in order to explain and admire its effectiveness. He explains that before he sets about swindling his audiences he establishes his authority and credibility by displaying a range of official documents, most if not all of them forgeries. His voice is loud and assertive, and what he has to say is well rehearsed. That the content of his preaching is carefully calculated is confirmed by the image of a cook preparing a recipe used to describe his insertion of a few words of Latin:

> And in Latyn I speke a wordes fewe,
> To saffron with my predicacioun,
> And for to stire hem to devocioun.
>
> (ll.344–346)

In his preaching he makes use of 'olde stories', because they appeal to 'lewed' (ignorant, uneducated) people who find them easy to remember (ll.437–438). We see here the Pardoner's contempt for his congregations — a contempt that is also evident in the gloating dismissiveness of:

> I rekke nevere, whan that they been beryed,
> Though that hir soules goon a-blakeberyed!
>
> (ll.405–406)

A practical demonstration of the kinds of techniques that will be employed in the tale is provided by the Pardoner's recitation to the pilgrims of the sales-talk that accompanies the exhibition of his bogus relics (ll.352–388). The importance of humour in his preaching, for example, is indicated by the lines on jealousy (ll.366–371), especially the outrageous reference to a wife committing adultery with two or three priests. The conclusion of the speech, in which the Pardoner reveals one of his cleverest tricks, illustrates the intelligence with which he manipulates his audiences. He declares that he will not accept offerings from those who have on their consciences sins so terrible that they have not dared to confess them. Under the guise of refusing to accept money from certain members of his congregation, the Pardoner in fact increases his revenue, because in order to avoid appearing guilty of appalling sinfulness his listeners are likely to rush forward with their offerings. The prologue also gives us a striking visual impression of the Pardoner in his pulpit. He presents a compelling spectacle:

> Thanne peyne I me to strecche forth the nekke,
> And est and west upon the peple I bekke,
> As dooth a dowve sittynge on a berne.
> Myne handes and my tonge goon so yerne
> That it is joye to se my bisynesse.

(ll.395–399)

With his restless, energetic movements of the head and hands, the Pardoner is clearly a figure who demands attention. The quotation also illustrates the Pardoner's delight in his own expertise, while the image of the dove — traditionally the symbol of the Holy Spirit — gives the lines an additional ironic force. A few lines later the Pardoner uses a more appropriate image, that of a venomous snake, to describe his use of the pulpit to denounce his enemies: 'Thanne wol I stynge hym with my tonge smerte . . . Thus spitte I out my venym' (ll.413, 421). The target of these attacks is those who sought to expose the corruption of medieval pardoners ('folk that doon us displeasances'). As he repeatedly asserts, however, the usual motive for his preaching is covetousness, and the tale that he is about to tell the pilgrims will be an example of this, a tale 'Which I am wont to preche for to wynne' (ll.461).

This tale has barely begun before the Pardoner breaks away from the main narrative in order to discourse on the rioters' sins, attacking in turn gluttony, drunkenness, gambling and blasphemy. It is a remarkable piece of preaching, and demonstrates how the Pardoner retains his audience's attention and interest by clever variations of tone and content. It is also the part of the poem which most obviously has the character of a medieval sermon. The discourse is packed with *ensamples*; the Pardoner's arguments are supported by references to the Bible, ancient history and Stoic philosophy. The biblical references are frequently made in an imperious tone which emphasises the

Pardoner's authority and erudition:

> And over al this, avyseth yow right wel
> What was comaunded unto Lamuel —
> Nat Samuel, but Lamuel, seye I;
> Redeth the Bible, and fynde it expresly
> Of wyn-yevyng to hem that han justise.
>
> (ll.583–587)

The Pardoner's use of the Bible itself illustrates the variety of his sermon. He includes solemn quotations from St Paul and Jeremiah, but, mindful of the need to give his preaching popular appeal, he also seizes on the dramatic and the lurid: Herod calling for John the Baptist's head, the drunken Lot sleeping with his two daughters. The Pardoner also appeals to his audience by incorporating into his discourse experiences that are a part of their everyday lives. He speaks of the wine merchants of Cheapside and Fish Street who, he says, cheat their customers by mixing cheap Spanish wine with more expensive varieties. The humorous tone of this passage continues when he describes the effect produced by this adulterated wine: after drinking three glasses of it a man will imagine that he is actually in Spain. Also comic is the description a few lines earlier of the drunkard's characteristic behaviour: his speech is slurred, he staggers about like a stuck pig and his heavy breathing is such that it sounds as if he is crying out, 'Sampsoun, Sampsoun!' (l.554). The vivid detail of this description illustrates how in the Pardoner's sermon the sins are not merely abstract entities but are given a convincing physical reality. The sections on drunkenness and gluttony in particular have this conviction, and Chaucer gives us the impression that it derives from the Pardoner's own experience — and enjoyment — of these sins. The Pardoner's drunkenness has already been hinted at in his Prologue, where he shamelessly declared 'I wol drynke licour of the vyne' (l.452), and in his insistence on a 'draughte of corny ale' before telling his tale. That he is also guilty of gluttony is suggested by the language he uses to describe it, which dwells on the pleasures of food and evokes with striking immediacy the physical sensation of eating:

> Out of the harde bones knokke they

The mary, for they caste noght awey
That may go thurgh the golet softe and swoote.
Of spicerie of leef, and bark, and roote
Shal been his sauce ymaked by delit,
To make hym yet a newer appetit.

(ll.541–546)

However, while the Pardoner may be attracted to the sins he is describing, he is at the same time capable of producing in his listeners a reaction of genuine revulsion:

O wombe! O bely! O stynkyng cod,
Fulfilled of dong and of corrupcioun!
At either ende of thee foul is the soun.

(ll.534–536)

O dronke man, disfigured is thy face,
Sour is thy breeth, foul artow to embrace

(ll.551–552)

Elsewhere in his digression the Pardoner's language is clearly intended to shock his audience — as when his preaching against blasphemy is accompanied by a string of blasphemous oaths. Another tactic is to dramatise the importance of each sin. Thus gluttony is the origin of man's damnation (because it induced Adam to eat the apple), blasphemy is the second of the Ten Commandments and therefore a worse sin than murder, and gambling is the:

. . . verray mooder of lesynges,
And of deceite, and cursed forswerynges,
Blaspheme of Crist, manslaughtre, and wast also
Of catel and of tyme

(ll.591–594)

It is characteristic of the Pardoner, as here, to present the sins of mankind as inextricably linked to one another: later he says again that gambling leads to 'Forsweryng, ire, falsnesse, homycide' (l.657), while drunkenness is said to stimulate lechery. This emphasis on the interrelationship of the sins offers further support to the Pardoner's central theme — that avarice is the *root* of all evils.

   Throughout his discourse the Pardoner demonstrates his

mastery of the rhetorical devices associated with medieval sermons. He makes use of repetition:

> The hooly writ take I to my witnesse
> That luxurie is in wyn and dronkenesse.

> (ll.483–484)

> A lecherous thyng is wyn . . .

> (l.549)

of onomatopoeia:

> As though thou seydest ay 'Sampsoun, Sampsoun!'

> (l.554)

and of exclamations:

> O glotonye, ful of cursednesse!
> O cause first of oure confusioun!
> O original of oure dampnacioun,
> Til Crist hadde boght us with his blood agayn!

> (l.498–501)

The *exclamatio* that regularly punctuate the Pardoner's digression increase the emotional impact of his sermon, helping to convince the audience of his sincerity and of the truth of his arguments.

The discourse continues for over 170 lines before the Pardoner signals that it has come to an end with the line: 'But, sires, now wol I telle forth my tale' (l.660). In the next line he returns briskly to the story of the rioters: 'Thise riotoures thre of whiche I telle'. The exemplum of the rioters' hunt for Death is the heart of the tale, but it is the discourse which precedes it that makes its function *as* an exemplum apparent. The rioters personify the sins the Pardoner has condemned (they drink, blaspheme and speak of gambling) and their story has the character of an allegory — the surface events of the narrative conceal a thinly veiled moral and spiritual meaning. The lengthy discussion of the sins at the beginning of the tale also means that once the main narrative has finally begun it is able to continue without further interruption: the rapid pace of the narrative has been widely recognised as one of its greatest strengths. The rioters seem to hurtle towards their own destruction, and the inevitability of their fate is highlighted. The tale's other qualities have also received frequent acknowledgement: the stark simplicity of setting, the rioters' naturalistic dialogue, the memorable contributions of figures such as the innkeeper and the serving-boy, the character of the old man with its strange, unsettling resonance.

The account of the rioters' deaths at the conclusion of the Pardoner's narrative is followed by further dramatic exclamations against the sins:

O cursed synne of alle cursednesse!
O traytours homycide, O wikkednesse!
O glotonye, luxurie and hasardrye!

(ll.895–897)

With the terrible fate of the rioters fresh in the minds of his listeners, the Pardoner's invocations now have an even greater emotional force. His fervour increases still further — indeed we imagine he may well be weeping by this stage — as he laments the treachery of mankind:

Allas, mankynde, how may it bitide
That to thy creatour, which that the wroghte,
And with his precious herte-blood thee boghte,
Thou art so fals and so unkynde, allas?

(ll.900–903)

After reiterating the theme of his preaching ('ware yow fro the synne of avarice!'), the Pardoner cleverly moves in for his financial killing, exploiting the impact of his story while his audience is still under its spell: 'Myn hooly pardoun may yow alle warice'. He promises to rid his listeners of their sins and guarantees them entry into 'the blisse of hevene' — in return, of course, for money (though he will also readily accept brooches, spoons, rings or wool). We are reminded of the true objective of the Pardoner's preaching: to induce a fear of sin so that his audience will want the absolution he claims he can provide and to induce a fear of avarice in particular so that they will more willingly part with their money. In a tone of unmistakable — if uncharacteristically muted — self-satisfaction the Pardoner concludes the demonstration of his skills:

And lo, sires, thus I preche.

1

How helpful to an understanding of *The Pardoner's Prologue and Tale* is an awareness of medieval preaching conventions?

2

How successful do you find the Pardoner's use of humour in his sermon?

3

Would you agree that the Pardoner's depiction of sins appears to be rooted in personal experience (page 91)?

4

How well does the Pardoner know his audience?

Pat Pinsent

Pat Pinsent is Principal Lecturer in English at the Roehampton Institute.

ESSAY

Narrative techniques in Chaucer's *Pardoner's Tale*

The most immediately striking quality of Chaucer's *Pardoner's Tale* is its unexpectedness. In response to the Host's request, 'Telle us som myrthe or japes right anon' (1.319)[1] the Pardoner, perhaps the most unpleasant, immoral and unlikeable pilgrim in the group, is attributed with one of the most moral tales in the collection.

The association of this tale with his confession, or more accurately, boast, about his duplicity and false relics, and his use of it to launch an appeal to his fellow-pilgrims to employ his services as a pardoner, has always intrigued readers. But these qualities alone would scarcely suffice to account for its significance and enduring popularity, if the story itself were of little interest.

It is my intention here to concentrate almost entirely on the narrative about the 'three rioters', paying some attention to the long digression early in the tale, but little to the framework of the Pardoner's own prologue or his attempt to sell his wares at

---

[1] See 'A note on the text' (p.8) regarding line references.

the end. This digression (ll.485–660), more than half the length of the tale itself, comes very shortly after the place — 'Flaundres' — and the characters — members of a 'compaignye' of young folk who indulge in many vices — have been introduced to us. The effect on the reader of this deviation from the narrative is likely to be one of inducing some impatience, and even the fear that even when we eventually start properly we may be delayed by another digression — a useful device for holding attention. As we later realise, it has other narrative functions. In its wandering from the path, it foreshadows the way the three revellers will later 'turne up this croked wey' (l.761) at the direction of the old man. More significantly, by devoting so much attention to the evil effects on biblical and historical characters of the vices of hazardry and gluttony, including drunkenness, it means that the flow of the main narrative where the characters display these vices need not be diverted for a denunciation at that point. It intensifies the feeling that such vices will inevitably lead to the downfall of the rioters, and so allows the author to be more economical then. All these vices can be seen as aspects of avarice, recalling to us the Pardoner's refrain, 'Radix malorum est Cupiditas' (ll.334, 426) (The love of money is the root of all evil). Ironically, and not to be forgotten by the reader, the Pardoner himself has just been drinking (l.328) and avarice is his own besetting sin.

The central story, of little more than 250 lines, has received high praise from critics. As Robinson notes in the Introduction to his edition of Chaucer,[2] 'His tale has sometimes been called the best short story in existence.' For this sort of praise to be given, the tale must exemplify the kind of qualities that are universally true of good stories. In this essay I will examine those qualities in the context of economy and pace, characterisation, style, and plot-form.

The shortness of the story is made possible by the fact that Chaucer avoids lengthy descriptions, of place, characters, or events. D V Harrington, in a paper entitled 'Narrative Speed in the *Pardoner's Tale*', suggests that the tale should be read

---

[2] *The Complete Works of Geoffrey Chaucer*, ed. F N Robinson, second edition (Oxford, 1968/85), p.11

rapidly in order to create the impression of events 'following hard upon each other'.[3] Thus the reader can be 'startled into a greater awareness by each successive scene', in a way more like the effect of a play than a poem. There is a minimum of description of scene, character or event. As I Bishop, in 'The Narrative Art of the *Pardoner's Tale*',[4] shows, the reader is prepared for the very concise ending ('What nedeth it to sermone of it moore? ...anon they storven bothe two' (ll.879–888)) by the relative abundance of detail given beforehand in the account of the planning of the murders. The elder rioters decide how to kill the youngest, and so it happens. The shopkeeper tells the youngest of the effects of the poison, and if we knew 'Avycen' (l.889) we would presumably need no more detail than Chaucer gives about the painful retribution they receive. Since this speed is largely attained by the use of speech, the technique may justly be termed dramatic. The audience are made to feel as if they are present, listening firstly to the Pardoner himself and then to the voices of the individual characters.

One of the strengths of the tale is the use of character. The three rioters are collectively portrayed in their use of 'many a grisly ooth' (l.708) and there is little or no individualisation of them, apart from one being the youngest (l.804) and another the worst (l.776). This in itself may be a strength of the story, as it means that no sympathy is wasted on them. We are more interested in their fate, which arises directly out of their evil: they need no external agent to kill them. Even while wasting no sympathy on them, we perhaps have a reluctant admiration for both plots, our sense of morality being preserved by the fact that we know none of the rioters can succeed. Again, the fact that the story is being told by a clever rogue himself adds to the complexity of our reaction.

The supporting characters are perhaps more individually portrayed than the main protagonists. This adds to the sense of verisimilitude — we have a picture of barely credible malignity set against a solid, tautly drawn, depiction of everyday life. The

---

[3] In *Twentieth Century Interpretations of the Pardoner's Tale*, ed. D W Faulkner (Englewood Cliffs, NJ, 1983), p. 35.

[4] In *Chaucer; The Canterbury Tales: A Casebook*, ed. J J Anderson (London, 1974).

boy, in his reliance on what he has been taught (1.684) and the host at the inn, who supports the boy's story by the detail about 'a greet village' (1.687) nearby, are ordinary people, like the apothecary, whose description of his wares (11.859–867) rings true. The old man seeking death has certainly attracted more controversy than the rest of the cast. He has a quality which no one else in the tale possesses; there is no reason to find him incredible as a human being, but he also acts as a symbol, intensifying the sense of fate. The additional threat of the pestilence (all too recent a folk memory for a post-Black Death Europe) heightens the sense of foreboding.

The way Chaucer's use of language adds to the effect of the narrative has already been touched on in part of the above discussion, and it is impossible here to exemplify it in the detail it deserves. The conviction of direct address of an audience, whether that of the pilgrims or the reader or hearer of the text, medieval or modern, is conveyed, as ever, by rhetorical devices, such as 'herkneth, lordynges' (1.573), 'Looke eek' (1.621). Particularly noteworthy is the resumption of the story proper, 'Thise riotoures thre of whiche I telle' (1.661). As well as waking us up and making us wonder if we have missed something — we have in fact not been told before how many rioters there were — it is an example of what Coghill calls 'the Possessive Demonstrative', which he suggests 'helps to bring his hearers onto the speaker's side' ('Chaucer's Narrative Art in *The Canterbury Tales*', *Chaucer and Chaucerians*, p. 135).

The aspects which I have considered above, economy and pace, characterisation and style, although very well displayed in *The Pardoner's Tale*, are in no way distinctive to it. Other examples could be adduced from other *Tales*. In order to justify the claims made for this one in particular, more is needed. At this point, then, in looking at the construction of the plot, I want to draw on its similarity with some of the other very short stories which continue to exert a hold on our imaginations, namely folk- and fairy-tales.

We know from the critics (Robinson in his Introduction to *The Complete Works of Geoffrey Chaucer*) of the affinity of the story with ancient folk-tales about the Buddha circulating in India from the fifth century BC. I have no desire to attempt to trace the origins of the underlying story nor if and how Chaucer might have been influenced by Asian material, but it is of interest to look at certain similarities with folk-tale type material far more familiar to most of us in Europe, the fairy-tales collected by Perrault, the Grimms, and Lang, all of whom wrote many centuries after Chaucer. There are many affinities in the use of certain narrative patterns and it may be that all these tales, which are of very ancient origin, have some elements which appeal universally to the human psyche. Perhaps the key one of these is the tension between predictability and surprise, the use of the reader's expectation balanced by enough variety so that the story doesn't become boring. Such elements are also common in the romances, verse and prose, so prolific in medieval England.

The summary of a fairly typical folk- or fairy-tale/romance might be: 'Once upon a time there were three brothers who went out into the world to seek their fortunes. They met an enchanter who told them that they would have to perform certain tasks. At the end of their quest, after considerable dangers, the youngest of them triumphed, received treasure, and probably married a princess. They lived happily ever after.'

Almost all the elements of this, except the happy ending and the optional princess, are present, but distorted, within *The Pardoner's Tale*. The setting is (relatively) distant, the time vague, 'whilom', meaning 'formerly or once'. There are three rioters, not brothers, but:

> Togidres han thise thre hir trouthes plight
> To lyve and dyen ech of hem for oother,
> As though he were his owene ybore brother.

(ll.702–705)

There is a mysterious old man who, while not inaugurating their quest to 'sleen this false traytour Deeth', does set them in the right direction for it. They all find treasure, which instead of being the object which makes them live 'happily ever after', causes them to find death and, presumably, hell. This is near enough in structure almost to suggest parody, but I think this is unlikely. What I think such parallels imply is that certain elements are frequent in the kind of short stories which are memorable and often form the framework for more elaborate treatments by major writers.

The reader's reaction to many of these elements is likely to be the blend of expectation and surprise which I have suggested is common in a good short story. Experienced readers and hearers of literature and of fairy-tale, know that something fateful will happen to the rioters because of the warnings about the vices in which they engage. The irrationality of a quest to slay Death is never commented on, suggesting, in this blend between a concrete and a vague setting, with no real names or precise timing, a story which is not exactly naturalistic but which is in no sense supernatural. Again, the experienced reader will be sure by now that the rioters *will* find death, but probably not in the way in which they expect.

The constant namelessness of the rioters and the fact that there are three of them induces in the reader of this poem a feeling rather like that of the reader of a fairy-tale. In particular, there is a strong tendency for identification with the youngest of any three, even among readers who themselves are elder siblings! While psychological reasons have been put forward for this, it is enough to think of the literary experience we, and presumably Chaucer's audience too, have gained from innumerable stories where the youngest is favoured. Thus when the youngest goes into the town and the others begin plotting against him, we have a natural movement of sympathy towards him, soon to be dispelled when he buys the poison!

Thus, throughout the tale the reader is in a state of divided reactions; we know what to expect, which makes us in a way superior to the participants, who are if anything too trusting. Would we have drunk the wine brought back from the town? Instead, however, of wanting to warn the elder two, we *want* them to meet their death through drinking it. Yet the kind of expectations generated by fairy-tale or romance material are not quite appropriate — there is no good character, no princess and no happy ending.

I think it is not accidental that there is so much in common between the structures of this short story and those anonymous ones which are part of our human heritage. This is not to suggest a deliberate use of any model by Chaucer, but rather his instinctive feel for what makes a good story.

Perhaps a significant reason for the success of the story is the way in which we feel that there is a power in control. This is attained by the craftsmanship with which Chaucer manipulates his ending, so that at one level we know he is in control, and at another, there is a force, Fate, or the Fortune which the rioters (l.779) mistakenly think has given them the treasure for their own delight. Although their deaths are not caused by any external force, the way in which their schemes are mutually destructive gives the reader the feeling of living in a just universe (at least within the tale!). In the light of this, we can be sure that the Pardoner himself will not get away with his own plans for fleecing his pilgrim audience and we fully endorse the Host's reaction: '"Nay, nay!" quod he, "thanne have I Cristes curs!"' (l.946). The Host's comment in fact reminds us of the excess of swearing by the rioters, and the fact that the Pardoner himself is, in a different way, taking God's name in vain by claiming to speak as a religious person when as a deceiver he is nearer the devil. Perhaps it would not be too fanciful to recognise Chaucer's technique here also, reminding his audience that God *is* in control and that in this case too, justice will be done.

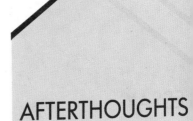

AFTERTHOUGHTS

1

What qualities do you think are essential to a good story?

2

Do you agree that supporting characters in *The Pardoner's Tale* are 'more individually portrayed than the main protagonists' (page 98)?

3

What similarities and differences does Pinsent highlight between *The Pardoner's Tale* and a traditional folk- or fairy-tale (pages 99–101)?

4

Do you agree that *The Pardoner's Tale* offers reassurance that we live 'in a just universe' (page 102)?

John E Cunningham

John E Cunningham currently divides his time between writing and travel. He is the author of numerous critical studies.

ESSAY

The Pardoner's Tale: an unholy mess?

Anyone who tried to get a first taste of Chaucer as a narrator by picking up this story might well be forgiven for wondering at his reputation. Such a reader would be faced by a tale that is in three divisions, almost in three styles: some 200 lines of opening denunciation of sin in a windy, rhetorical manner, based on the doings of a company of young people in Flanders with their attendant panders; a further, slightly longer section, which starts off with three drunkards in a pub and develops simply and starkly into a story of betrayal and death; then a shorter coda, at first in the manner of the opening, which turns into slick sales-patter and at last degenerates into an intervention of the rudest kind by the referee. The novice could be so put off by this apparent gallimaufry that the exploration would end there. How might we persuade the disappointed reader to persevere?

First of all it is worth looking a little more closely into the nature of the three sections that have been suggested, and then seeing if we can relate them to the man who tells them, as he is described in the *General Prologue* and in his own prologue. In so doing we may find a pattern not at first apparent.

The Pardoner pitches straight into the middle of what is seemingly his story, with a 'company' of young people who drink and swear and gamble, who are attended by dancing-girls and

fruit-sellers, bawds and cake-vendors, and generally appear to
be having a very good time. Then he turns aside from this theme
and starts to give what his audience would recognise as a
standard device of rhetoric, a series of examples of drunkenness
and lust. These examples are very muddled to our way of
thinking, and some of them hardly seem to fit: what his daughters got up to with Lot when he was drunk was hardly his fault;
Adam does not strike us as an example of gluttony, rather of
disobedience; or, if we must keep to the strict list of the Seven
Deadly Sins, of pride in thinking that he knew better than God
what was good for him. The catalogue has hardly begun when it
is interrupted by another well-worn device of the public speaker
of those times, the apostrophe: a turning away from the main
line of the speech to address some person, some sin or, as here
rather absurdly, some sinful organ — 'O wombe! O bely! O
stynkyng cod' (1.534).[1] There follow some reflections on which
sort of wine is the most intoxicating — a topic on which the
Pardoner speaks with the authority of a man who was drunk
when he started — and then he swings back to his examples:
swings indeed might describe the wild range which takes in
Attila the Hun, a Spartan ambassador, a little-known figure
from the Book of Proverbs and Demetrius of Parthia. Then he
descends to common language and gives us a sudden chance to
hear medieval speech as it really was, quoting the oaths of the
gambling den:

> ... 'By the blood of Crist that is in Hayles,
> Sevene is my chaunce, and thyn is cynk and treye!'
>
> (ll.652–653)

Then, with an abrupt remark that he will get on with his story,
he switches his style completely, with 'Thise riotoures thre of
whiche I telle' (1.661) though he had *not* been talking about a
threesome, but a considerable party with a whole retinue of
pleasure; but these three men — not, it seems, particularly
young — are sitting in a pub with only one attendant, a boy who
is sent to ask what the bell is ringing for.

However, the development of the second section would surely

---

[1] See 'A note on the text' (p. 8) regarding line references.

strike any new reader as being well done, though it has to be read carefully to see just how well. It has a deceptive simplicity such as we find in the best-known traditional tales. The men are never even given names, but are distinguished well enough: the eldest is the worst, the middle one the most suggestible, the youngest capable of executing the deepest treachery on his own. The rapid run of the narrative, starting with the drunken and noisy resolution to conquer Death, is checked by the episode of the old man. They curse him in a series of blasphemies that recalls the oaths of the gambling table, and treat him with none of the respect which is due to his age. He answers them gravely and tells them that to him Death, whom they would destroy, would be welcome, a kindly mother to whom he would return. He echoes the sentiment found on many tombs of the period, whose burden, often in epigrammatic Latin, is: I was once as you are now — you will be as I am. But he directs them — they will find Death, he says, up 'this croked wey' and he will wait for their coming. What follows unrolls with the relentlessness of tragedy. Their delight in finding the money is tempered by the fear that they may not be able to enjoy it. The plausibility of the proposal put forward by the eldest matches its duplicity, revealed as soon as the youngest has gone on his errand. He in turn spins a typically embroidered tale about a polecat to get the poison, and the apothecary, a neat picture of a professional, gives solemn warning of the fatal power of his wares, soon to be displayed to us. There is a last touch of heartlessness in that the other two, their brutal murder done, propose to sit and drink and make merry before they bury the body of their erstwhile comrade, and we are then given a gruesome account of their final sufferings. We might expect the story to end there, for its point is made as we see the picture of the three bodies by their useless trove. Death waited for them to come all right.

Here, however, the Pardoner reverts to his earlier manner, with a noisy apostrophe which seems as muddled as it is spuriously indignant, bundling homicide, gluttony, lust and dicing into a rag-bag of denunciation. This short outburst done, he turns to his audience and with yet another change of tone briskly tells them that he can offer them absolution for their sins, and that he has relics as well as pardons in his bag. Indeed he says he can offer them a sort of continuous insurance during the hazards of the journey, and suggests, with remarkable lack of judgement, that the Host, being corpulent and thus more liable to the sins of the flesh, should be the first penitent. Annoyed at this personal remark, the Host responds with interest: he would like, he says, to make a holy relic of that part of the Pardoner which, we were told in the *General Prologue*, the Pardoner no longer has, if he ever did. The sexual insult is so shrewd that he becomes speechless with rage:

> So wrooth he was, no worde ne wolde he seye
>
> (1.957)

and the Knight is forced to act as a peace-maker. So ends *The Pardoner's Tale*.

Our first attempt to resolve these disparate elements may begin by taking up this insult. The Pardoner is the last pilgrim to be described, if we except the Host, in the *General Prologue* (I, ll.669–714). He rides with the Summoner, and a precious pair they make; the latter with his spotty face and stinking breath, the former with his scanty hair spread over his shoulders in what he thinks is the latest style and singing in an unbroken voice some love-song of the day, to which the Summoner provides a bass part. What they have in common is that they are corrupt servants of the Church, the Summoner taking bribes and promoting the very moral mischief he should report to the ecclesiastical court, the Pardoner making money, his whole preoccupation, out of relics which are manifestly false. But he is good at his job. The treble voice, whose cause is the same lack of manhood that gives him a beardless cheek and the grounds for the Host's riposte, can sing an offertory well — and also, in a key passage, we are told:

> Wel koude he rede a lessoun or a storie
> >   . . . whan that song was songe,
> He moste preche and wel affile his tonge
> To wynne silver, as he ful wel koude
>
> (I, ll.709, 711–713)

We have already been told that when he met a poor parson of a remote country district he could make more money out of him and his congregation than the parson earned in two months. There is one such parson amongst the pilgrims and his tale consists of a sermon with which Chaucer intended to conclude the immense fabric of stories — 120 in all — that he did not live to complete. How does the Pardoner's preaching compare with that of the poor Parson, who is, unusually perhaps, a university graduate? Can we, by such a comparison, evaluate the Pardoner's pulpit style?

Few modern readers have the tenacity to read the lengthy discourse with which Chaucer was to end the *Tales*, though it is in a plain enough style. The Parson first talks about the need for true penitence — very different from the cash-and-carry or credit-card systems advocated by the Pardoner — then he gives a thorough analysis of the nature of each of the Seven Deadly Sins, together with ways in which they may be countered. He quotes the Pardoner's own text — *Radix malorum est Cupiditas* — and agrees with him that this is the greatest sin of all. He also condemns those avaricious persons, who, like the Pardoner and Summoner, destroy the Church from within for their own greedy purposes. He ends with a moving picture of the joy which may be attained through genuine repentance:

> This blisful regne may men purchace by poverte espiritueel,
> and the glorie by lowenesse, the plentee of joye by hunger
> and thurst, and the reste by travaille, and the lyf by deeth
> and the mortificacion of synne.

(X, l.1080)

This grave but happy conclusion is far from the Pardoner's noisy denunciations and opportunist sales-talk. This bliss is to be 'purchaced' not by cash but by spiritual discipline.

If the Pardoner's sermon has something in common with the Parson's, it is the use of examples; but the Parson's are always clearly appropriate where the Pardoner's are not always obviously so. The Parson's whole approach is far from being rhetorical; it is careful and measured. Ordinary people tend to like something more robust, appealing more to their feelings than to their minds, and we may suppose that the Pardoner is the kind of dramatic preacher whose sermons the rackety Wife of Bath loved to go and hear. But she begins *her* story by condemning preachers who twist texts to their own ends, and devious ingenuity may be detected in the Pardoner's methods: perhaps his opening passage is intended as an illustration of how a fundamentally dishonest preacher could nevertheless capture a popular hearing by sheer energy and guile: for Adam was not, as he says, driven out of Paradise for gluttony — but he certainly ate something; that Herod was drunk when he ordered the execution of John is simply made up — but Herod was a medieval bogeyman on whom any vice could be fixed; the moral connection between drinking and gambling is unclear, but as one is often associated with the other he can take an easy swipe at the gaming-table; Old and New Testament texts are dragged in to condemn swearing, though their real point seems to be that an oath should be a reliable promise. All is grist to the Pardoner's busy mill, and the old showbiz adage — they liked it once, they'll love it twice — might have been coined for him. As he explains in his own prologue:

> Thus kan I preche agayn that same vice
> Which that I use, and that is avarice.
>
> (ll.427–429)

Avarice: are we to assume that in his treatment of his main theme he is as wilfully confused as in his examples? Here he is on surer ground. Avarice is not one of the Seven Deadly Sins, amongst which its nearest relative is Covetousness; and Gluttony, which he often treats as if it were the same as Avarice, is in fact one of them: but to the medieval mind the Latin word *cupiditas* — for which the modern 'cupidity' is a poor and laborious equivalent — was something much broader than the 'love of money' which exactly translates Paul's original Greek. It was the opposite to *caritas* — again the modern 'charity' is inadequate: these were the two types of love, earthly and heavenly, the love that grabbed for itself and the love that gave all, asking nothing. *Cupiditas* covered greed for money, sexual lust, love of food and drink, in fact any form of inordinate desire. The Pardoner is quite entitled to bring a wide range of sins under this umbrella, insincere though the wretch is. And he might have argued that he was also entitled to use any cheap dodges of rhetoric, such as the raucous apostrophes, to succeed in his preaching.

But we are told, in lines already quoted, not only that he could preach well, but that he knew well how to read a lesson or a story. This may refer to stories of the lives of saints, but it is tempting to think that it also means he sometimes read a parable, for this, surely, is what the story of Death and the rioters really is: told, as are the great parables, and the most enduring of folk-tales too, with simplicity and effect; universal in language and appeal; little affected by the passage of time, even if Death would suggest to the medieval hearer 'The Black Death', the plague that came back each summer to kill off its thousands irrespective of rank or age or virtue: as, after all, thousands of us are killed each year by mere impatience on the roads.

The change from pulpit-thumping to story-telling is, then, not unprepared: nor is the later switch to sales-talk. The Pardoner errs only in supposing the pilgrims had forgotten what he had already told them of his ability in the field of the hard sell.

His technique is explained quite openly, even with pride, in his prologue. He says that he begins by a display of his credentials, his papal documents. Then his wares are revealed, each with a sales spiel about its particular powers. There is even a special offer: the relics are open only to those who are free of fear of shame — others will find themselves powerless to make an offering. What listener could resist showing his or her lack of guilt? And, he avers, he tells them 'an hundred false japes moore' (l.394).

The success of his dishonest sales was assured by the fear that underlay the whole business of the granting of indulgences. Though belief in purgatory did not become an article of faith until 1439, the idea of a place of punishment to which all but the saints must go for a prolonged period of severe suffering had been current since it was promulgated by Gregory and Augustine some 800 years earlier. The possibility which indulgences offered — of buying time off, in advance, for cash — had already led to such abuses that, at about the time this tale was written, Pope Boniface IX was obliged to condemn them officially; but they continued until the impudent money-raising of Jonathan Tetzel, a century later, provoked Luther to his revolt and so led to the Reformation. While Chaucer seems to have been a true son of the Church, he was not blind to its corruptions, and shows his feelings here and elsewhere — there is a sharp awareness in his picture of the worldly Monk, for example.

In that picture, as here, he shows his keen sense and subtle use of irony. The supreme irony of the Pardoner is that in the teller himself all the related themes of the tale are presented: drunkenness — already tipsy, he asks for yet another drink before he starts; avarice, which he confesses is his own chief motive in all that he does; and the associated sin of anger, the mainspring of the murders in the story, the blind fury against death itself, the irate abuse of the old man, which the Pardoner shows when he is insulted by the Host.

So it is ironic — but not impossible — that the Pardoner should denounce the very vice that is his passion; it is ironic — but not unthinkable — that he should reveal his own guile to the pilgrims, but later, carried away by his own eloquence, slip back into his familiar patter as a seller of pardons; it is ironic, but surely acceptable, that he can indulge in windy flights of dubious rhetoric, like every successful demagogue before and since, yet be capable of a simple and effective narration. Most of us, after all, know how to adopt more than one manner of speech for different purposes.

Nor are the two 'voices' without connections. The Pardoner may not follow the elaborate patterns of a medieval sermon like the Parson's, with introduction, divisions, subdivisions and conclusion; but he does state his theme — announces it by denouncing it, indeed — then illustrates it in a fine anecdote, and recapitulates it before trying to cash in for himself. He follows the advice still often given to public speakers: tell them what you are going to say; say it; then tell them what you have said.

If this formula is still current, what of his story? The oral tradition, in which Chaucer's work flourished, which made sermons good entertainment, may have passed into a culture that is more dependent on the written word and the televised image, but a well-told story, such as that of Death and the rioters, still has the power to hold attention. Nor are the rhetorical flourishes which introduce and follow it quite extinct. With a fiery sincerity — which he so notably lacks — they may still echo from Welsh and Northern Irish pulpits, where the power of the spoken word is admired and cultivated; and they resound in the televised evangelism of America, ring out in the fervour of the Bible Belt.

Far from bundling up two or three different fragments and styles, Chaucer has presented us with a careful package of tale and teller, and one that can still provoke us to thought as we seek to unwrap it.

AFTERTHOUGHTS

1

How disruptive or otherwise do you find the 'divisions' (page 104) in *The Pardoner's Tale*?

2

What 'cheap dodges of rhetoric' (page 109) does Cunningham identify in *The Pardoner's Tale*?

3

Explain the importance to this essay of the comparison of *The Parson's Tale* with *The Pardoner's Tale*.

4

What characteristics link the Pardoner with a contemporary salesman?

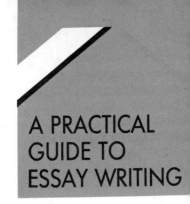

A PRACTICAL GUIDE TO ESSAY WRITING

INTRODUCTION

First, a word of warning. Good essays are the product of a creative engagement with literature. So never try to restrict your studies to what you think will be 'useful in the exam'. Ironically, you will restrict your grade potential if you do.

This doesn't mean, of course, that you should ignore the basic skills of essay writing. When you read critics, make a conscious effort to notice *how* they communicate their ideas. The guidelines that follow offer advice of a more explicit kind. But they are no substitute for practical experience. It is never easy to express ideas with clarity and precision. But the more often you tackle the problems involved and experiment to find your own voice, the more fluent you will become. So practise writing essays as often as possible.

HOW TO PLAN
AN ESSAY

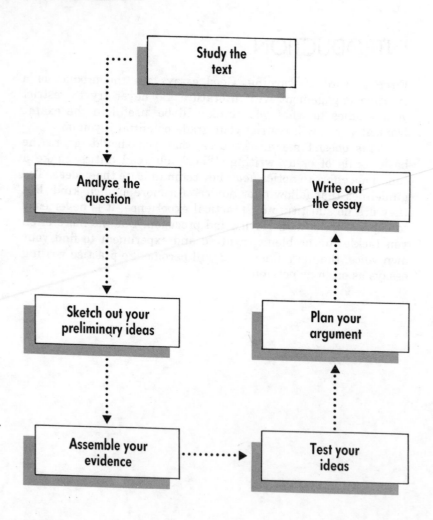

Study the text

Analyse the question

Write out the essay

Sketch out your preliminary ideas

Plan your argument

Assemble your evidence

Test your ideas

Study the text

The first step in writing a good essay is to get to know the set text well. Never write about a text until you are fully familiar with it. Even a discussion of the opening chapter of a novel, for example, should be informed by an understanding of the book as a whole. Literary texts, however, are by their very nature complex and on a first reading you are bound to miss many significant features. Re-read the book with care, if possible more than once. Look up any unfamiliar words in a good dictionary and if the text you are studying was written more than a few decades ago, consult the *Oxford English Dictionary* to find out whether the meanings of any terms have shifted in the intervening period.

Good books are difficult to put down when you first read them. But a more leisurely second or third reading gives you the opportunity to make notes on those features you find significant. An index of characters and events is often useful, particularly when studying novels with a complex plot or time scheme. The main aim, however, should be to record your *responses* to the text. By all means note, for example, striking images. But be sure to add *why* you think them striking. Similarly, record any thoughts you may have on interesting comparisons with other texts, puzzling points of characterisation, even what you take to be aesthetic blemishes. The important thing is to annotate fully and adventurously. The most seemingly idiosyncratic comment may later lead to a crucial area of discussion which you would otherwise have overlooked. It helps to have a working copy of the text in which to mark up key passages and jot down marginal comments (although obviously these practices are taboo when working with library, borrowed or valuable copies!). But keep a fuller set of notes as well and organise these under appropriate headings.

Literature does not exist in an aesthetic vacuum, however, and you should try to find out as much as possible about the context of its production and reception. It is particularly important to read other works by the same author and writings by contemporaries. At this early stage, you may want to restrict your secondary reading to those standard reference works, such as biographies, which are widely available in public libraries. In the long run, however, it pays to read as wide a range of critical studies as possible.

Some students, and tutors, worry that such studies may stifle the development of any truly personal response. But this won't happen if you are alert to the danger and read critically. After all, you wouldn't passively accept what a stranger told you in conversation. The fact that a critic's views are in print does not necessarily make them any more authoritative (as a glance at the review pages of the *TLS* and *London Review of Books* will reveal). So question the views you find: 'Does this critic's interpretation agree with mine and where do we part company?' 'Can it be right to try and restrict this text's meanings to those found by its author or first audience?' 'Doesn't this passage treat a theatrical text as though it were a novel?' Often it is views which you reject which prove most valuable since they challenge you to articulate your own position with greater clarity. Be sure to keep careful notes on what the critic wrote, and your *reactions* to what the critic wrote.

Analyse the question

You cannot begin to answer a question until you understand what task it is you have been asked to perform. Re-cast the question in your own words and reconstruct the line of reasoning which lies behind it. Where there is a choice of topics, try to choose the one for which you are best prepared. It would, for example, be unwise to tackle 'How far do you agree that in *Paradise Lost* Milton transformed the epic models he inherited from ancient Greece and Rome?' without a working knowledge of Homer and Virgil (or *Paradise Lost* for that matter!). If you do not already know the works of these authors, the question should spur you on to read more widely — or discourage you from attempting it at all. The scope of an essay, however, is not always so obvious and you must remain alert to the implied demands of each question. How could you possibly 'Consider the view that *Wuthering Heights* transcends the conventions of the Gothic novel' without reference to at least some of those works which, the question suggests, have *not* transcended Gothic conventions?

When you have decided on a topic, analyse the terms of the question itself. Sometimes these self-evidently require careful definition: *tragedy* and *irony*, for example, are notoriously difficult concepts to pin down and you will probably need to consult a good dictionary of literary terms. Don't ignore, however, those seemingly innocuous phrases which often smuggle in significant assumptions. 'Does Macbeth lack the nobility of the true tragic hero?' obviously invites you to discuss nobility and the nature of the tragic hero. But what of 'lack' and 'true' — do they suggest that the play would be improved had Shakespeare depicted Macbeth in a different manner? or that tragedy is superior to other forms of drama? Remember that you are not expected meekly to agree with the assumptions implicit in the question. Some questions are deliberately provocative in order to stimulate an engaged response. Don't be afraid to take up the challenge.

Sketch out your preliminary ideas

'Which comes first, the evidence or the answer?' is one of those chicken and egg questions. How can you form a view without inspecting the evidence? But how can you know which evidence is relevant without some idea of what it is you are looking for? In practice the mind reviews evidence and formulates preliminary theories or hypotheses at one and the same time, although for the sake of clarity we have separated out the processes. Remember that these early ideas are only there to get you started. You *expect* to modify them in the light of the evidence you uncover. Your initial hypothesis may be an instinctive 'gut-reaction'. Or you may find that you prefer to 'sleep on the problem', allowing ideas to gell over a period of time. Don't worry in either case. The mind is quite capable of processing a vast amount of accumulated evidence, the product of previous reading and thought, and reaching sophisticated intuitive judgements. Eventually, however, you are going to have to think carefully through any ideas you arrive at by such intuitive processes. Are they logical? Do they take account of all the relevant factors? Do they fully answer the question set? Are there any obvious reasons to qualify or abandon them?

Assemble your evidence

Now is the time to return to the text and re-read it with the question and your working hypothesis firmly in mind. Many of the notes you have already made are likely to be useful, but assess the precise relevance of this material and make notes on any new evidence you discover. The important thing is to cast your net widely and take into account points which tend to undermine your case as well as those that support it. As always, ensure that your notes are full, accurate, and reflect your own critical judgements.

You may well need to go outside the text if you are to do full justice to the question. If you think that the 'Oedipus complex' may be relevant to an answer on *Hamlet* then read Freud and a balanced selection of those critics who have discussed the appropriateness of applying psychoanalytical theories to the interpretation of literature. Their views can most easily be tracked down by consulting the annotated bibliographies held by most major libraries (and don't be afraid to ask a librarian for help in finding and using these). Remember that you go to works of criticism not only to obtain information but to stimulate you into clarifying your own position. And that since life is short and many critical studies are long, judicious use of a book's index and/or contents list is not to be scorned. You can save yourself a great deal of future labour if you carefully record full bibliographic details at this stage.

Once you have collected the evidence, organise it coherently. Sort the detailed points into related groups and identify the quotations which support these. You must also assess the relative importance of each point, for in an essay of limited length it is essential to establish a firm set of priorities, exploring some ideas in depth while discarding or subordinating others.

Test your ideas

As we stressed earlier, a hypothesis is only a proposal, and one that you fully expect to modify. Review it with the evidence before you. Do you really still believe in it? It would be surprising if you did not want to modify it in some way. If you cannot see any problems, others may. Try discussing your ideas with friends and relatives. Raise them in class discussions. Your tutor is certain to welcome your initiative. The critical process is essentially collaborative and there is absolutely no reason why you should not listen to and benefit from the views of others. Similarly, you should feel free to test your ideas against the theories put forward in academic journals and books. But do not just borrow what you find. Critically analyse the views on offer and, where appropriate, integrate them into your own pattern of thought. You must, of course, give full acknowledgement to the sources of such views.

Do not despair if you find you have to abandon or modify significantly your initial position. The fact that you are prepared to do so is a mark of intellectual integrity. Dogmatism is never an academic virtue and many of the best essays explore the *process* of scholarly enquiry rather than simply record its results.

Plan your argument

Once you have more or less decided on your attitude to the question (for an answer is never really 'finalised') you have to present your case in the most persuasive manner. In order to do this you must avoid meandering from point to point and instead produce an organised argument — a structured flow of ideas and supporting evidence, leading logically to a conclusion which fully answers the question. Never begin to write until you have produced an outline of your argument.

You may find it easiest to begin by sketching out its main stages as a flow chart or some other form of visual presentation. But eventually you should produce a list of paragraph topics. The paragraph is the conventional written demarcation for a unit of thought and you can outline an argument quite simply by briefly summarising the substance of each paragraph and then checking that these points (you may remember your English teacher referring to them as topic sentences) really do follow a coherent order. Later you will be able to elaborate on each topic, illustrating and qualifying it as you go along. But you will find this far easier to do if you possess from the outset a clear map of where you are heading.

All questions require some form of an argument. Even so-called 'descriptive' questions *imply* the need for an argument. An adequate answer to the request to 'Outline the role of Iago in *Othello*' would do far more than simply list his appearances on stage. It would at the very least attempt to provide some *explanation* for his actions — is he, for example, a representative stage 'Machiavel'? an example of pure evil, 'motiveless malignity'? or a realistic study of a tormented personality reacting to identifiable social and psychological pressures?

Your conclusion ought to address the terms of the question. It may seem obvious, but 'how far do you agree', 'evaluate', 'consider', 'discuss', etc, are *not* interchangeable formulas and your conclusion must take account of the precise wording of the question. If asked 'How far do you agree?', the concluding paragraph of your essay really should state whether you are in complete agreement, total disagreement, or, more likely, partial agreement. Each preceding paragraph should have a clear justification for its existence and help to clarify the reasoning which underlies your conclusion. If you find that a paragraph serves no good purpose (perhaps merely summarising the plot), do not hesitate to discard it.

The arrangement of the paragraphs, the overall strategy of the argument, can vary. One possible pattern is dialectical: present the arguments in favour of one point of view (**thesis**); then turn to counter-arguments or to a rival interpretation (**antithesis**); finally evaluate the competing claims and arrive at your own conclusion (**synthesis**). You may, on the other hand, feel so convinced of the merits of one particular case that you wish to devote your entire essay to arguing that viewpoint persuasively (although it is always desirable to indicate, however briefly, that you are aware of alternative, if flawed, positions). As the essays contained in this volume demonstrate, there are many other possible strategies. Try to adopt the one which will most comfortably accommodate the demands of the question and allow you to express your thoughts with the greatest possible clarity.

Be careful, however, not to apply abstract formulas in a mechanical manner. It is true that you should be careful to define your terms. It is *not* true that every essay should begin with 'The dictionary defines *x* as . . .'. In fact, definitions are often best left until an appropriate moment for their introduction arrives. Similarly every essay should have a beginning, middle and end. But it does not follow that in your opening paragraph you should announce an intention to write an essay, or that in your concluding paragraph you need to signal an imminent desire to put down your pen. The old adages are often useful reminders of what constitutes good practice, but they must be interpreted intelligently.

Write out the essay

Once you have developed a coherent argument you should aim to communicate it in the most effective manner possible. Make certain you clearly identify yourself, and the question you are answering. Ideally, type your answer, or at least ensure your handwriting is legible and that you leave sufficient space for your tutor's comments. Careless presentation merely distracts from the force of your argument. Errors of grammar, syntax and spelling are far more serious. At best they are an irritating blemish, particularly in the work of a student who should be sensitive to the nuances of language. At worst, they seriously confuse the sense of your argument. If you are aware that you have stylistic problems of this kind, ask your tutor for advice at the earliest opportunity. Everyone, however, is liable to commit the occasional howler. The only remedy is to give yourself plenty of time in which to proof-read your manuscript (often reading it aloud is helpful) before submitting it.

Language, however, is not only an instrument of communication; it is also an instrument of thought. If you want to think clearly and precisely you should strive for a clear, precise prose style. Keep your sentences short and direct. Use modern, straightforward English wherever possible. Avoid repetition, clichés and wordiness. Beware of generalisations, simplifications, and overstatements. Orwell analysed the relationship between stylistic vice and muddled thought in his essay 'Politics and the English Language' (1946) — it remains essential reading (and is still readily available in volume 4 of the Penguin *Collected Essays, Journalism and Letters*). Generalisations, for example, are always dangerous. They are rarely true and tend to suppress the individuality of the texts in question. A remark such as 'Keats always employs sensuous language in his poetry' is not only fatuous (what, after all, does it mean? is *every* word he wrote equally 'sensuous'?) but tends to obscure interesting distinctions which could otherwise be made between, say, the descriptions in the 'Ode on a Grecian Urn' and those in 'To Autumn'.

The intelligent use of quotations can help you make your points with greater clarity. Don't sprinkle them throughout your essay without good reason. There is no need, for example, to use them to support uncontentious statements of fact. 'Macbeth murdered Duncan' does not require textual evidence (unless you wish to dispute Thurber's brilliant parody, 'The Macbeth Murder Mystery', which reveals Lady Macbeth's father as the culprit!). Quotations should be included, however, when they are necessary to support your case. The proposition that Macbeth's imaginative powers wither after he has killed his king would certainly require extensive quotation: you would almost certainly want to analyse key passages from both before and after the murder (perhaps his first and last soliloquies?). The key word here is 'analyse'. Quotations cannot make your points on their own. It is up to you to demonstrate their relevance and clearly explain to your readers *why* you want them to focus on the passage you have selected.

Most of the academic conventions which govern the presentation of essays are set out briefly in the style sheet below. The question of gender, however, requires fuller discussion. More than half the population of the world is female. Yet many writers still refer to an undifferentiated *man*kind. Or write of the author and *his* public. We do not think that this convention has much to recommend it. At the very least, it runs the risk of introducing unintended sexist attitudes. And at times leads to such patent absurdities as 'Cleopatra's final speech asserts *man*'s true nobility'. With a little thought, you can normally find ways of expressing yourself which do not suggest that the typical author, critic or reader is male. Often you can simply use plural forms, which is probably a more elegant solution than relying on such awkward formulations as 's/he' or 'he and she'. You should also try to avoid distinguishing between male and female authors on the basis of forenames. Why *Jane* Austen and not *George* Byron? Refer to all authors by their last names unless there is some good reason not to. Where there may otherwise be confusion, say between T S and George Eliot, give the name in full when if first occurs and thereafter use the last name only.

Finally, keep your audience firmly in mind. Tutors and examiners are interested in understanding your conclusions and the processes by which you arrived at them. They are not interested in reading a potted version of a book they already know. **So don't pad out your work with plot summary.**

Hints for examinations

In an examination you should go through exactly the same processes as you would for the preparation of a term essay. The only difference lies in the fact that some of the stages will have had to take place before you enter the examination room. This should not bother you unduly. Examiners are bound to avoid the merely eccentric when they come to formulate papers and if you have read widely and thought deeply about the central issues raised by your set texts you can be confident you will have sufficient material to answer the majority of questions sensibly.

The fact that examinations impose strict time limits makes it *more* rather than less, important that you plan carefully. There really is no point in floundering into an answer without any idea of where you are going, particularly when there will not be time to recover from the initial error.

Before you begin to answer any question at all, study the entire paper with care. Check that you understand the rubric and know how many questions you have to answer and whether any are compulsory. It may be comforting to spot a title you feel confident of answering well, but don't rush to tackle it: read *all* the questions before deciding which *combination* will allow you to display your abilities to the fullest advantage. Once you have made your choice, analyse each question, sketch out your ideas, assemble the evidence, review your initial hypothesis, plan your argument, *before* trying to write out an answer. And make notes at each stage: not only will these help you arrive at a sensible conclusion, but examiners are impressed by evidence of careful thought.

Plan your time as well as your answers. If you have practised writing timed essays as part of your revision, you should not find this too difficult. There can be a temptation to allocate extra time to the questions you know you can answer well; but this is always a short-sighted policy. You will find yourself left to face a question which would in any event have given you difficulty without even the time to give it serious thought. It is, moreover, easier to gain marks at the lower end of the scale than at the upper, and you will never compensate for one poor answer by further polishing two satisfactory answers. Try to leave some time at the end of the examination to re-read your answers and correct any obvious errors. If the worst comes to the worst and you run short of time, don't just keep writing until you are forced to break off in mid-paragraph. It is far better to provide for the examiner a set of notes which indicate the overall direction of your argument.

Good luck — but if you prepare for the examination conscientiously and tackle the paper in a methodical manner, you won't need it!

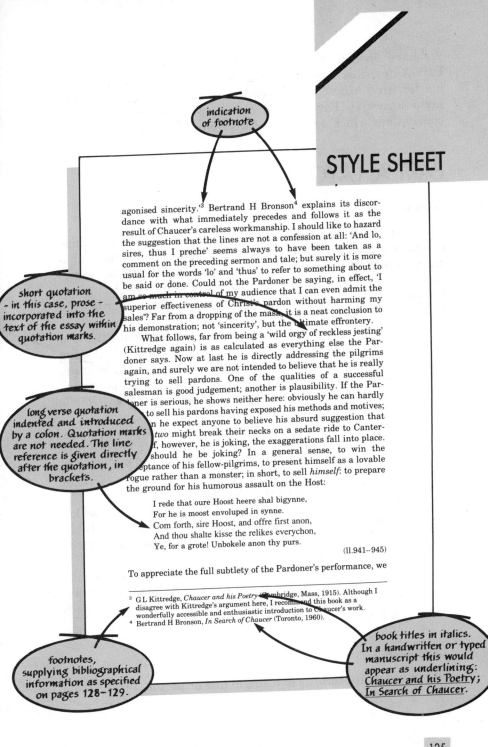

STYLE SHEET

indication of footnote

agonised sincerity.'[3] Bertrand H Bronson[4] explains its discordance with what immediately precedes and follows it as the result of Chaucer's careless workmanship. I should like to hazard the suggestion that the lines are not a confession at all: 'And lo, sires, thus I preche' seems always to have been taken as a comment on the preceding sermon and tale; but surely it is more usual for the words 'lo' and 'thus' to refer to something about to be said or done. Could not the Pardoner be saying, in effect, 'I am so much in control of my audience that I can even admit the superior effectiveness of Christ's pardon without harming my sales'? Far from a dropping of the mask, it is a neat conclusion to his demonstration; not 'sincerity', but the ultimate effrontery.

short quotation – in this case, prose – incorporated into the text of the essay within quotation marks.

What follows, far from being a 'wild orgy of reckless jesting' (Kittredge again) is as calculated as everything else the Pardoner says. Now at last he is directly addressing the pilgrims again, and surely we are not intended to believe that he is really trying to sell pardons. One of the qualities of a successful salesman is good judgement; another is plausibility. If the Pardoner is serious, he shows neither here: obviously he can hardly hope to sell his pardons having exposed his methods and motives; can he expect anyone to believe his absurd suggestion that the two might break their necks on a sedate ride to Canterbury? If, however, he is joking, the exaggerations fall into place. Why should he be joking? In a general sense, to win the acceptance of his fellow-pilgrims, to present himself as a lovable rogue rather than a monster; in short, to sell *himself*: to prepare the ground for his humorous assault on the Host:

long verse quotation indented and introduced by a colon. Quotation marks are not needed. The line reference is given directly after the quotation, in brackets.

> I rede that oure Hoost heere shal bigynne,
> For he is moost envoluped in synne.
> Com forth, sire Hoost, and offre first anon,
> And thou shalte kisse the relikes everychon,
> Ye, for a grote! Unbokele anon thy purs.
>
> (ll.941–945)

To appreciate the full subtlety of the Pardoner's performance, we

---

[3] G L Kittredge, *Chaucer and his Poetry* (Cambridge, Mass, 1915). Although I disagree with Kittredge's argument here, I recommend this book as a wonderfully accessible and enthusiastic introduction to Chaucer's work.
[4] Bertrand H Bronson, *In Search of Chaucer* (Toronto, 1960).

footnotes, supplying bibliographical information as specified on pages 128–129.

book titles in italics. In a handwritten or typed manuscript this would appear as underlining: Chaucer and his Poetry; In Search of Chaucer.

We have divided the following information into two sections. Part A describes those rules which it is essential to master no matter what kind of essay you are writing (including examination answers). Part B sets out some of the more detailed conventions which govern the documentation of essays.

PART A: LAYOUT

Titles of texts

Titles of published books, plays (of any length), long poems, pamphlets and periodicals (including newspapers and magazines), works of classical literature, and films should be underlined: e.g. David Copperfield (novel), Twelfth Night (play), Paradise Lost (long poem), Critical Quarterly (periodical), Horace's Ars Poetica (Classical work), Apocalypse Now (film).

Notice how important it is to distinguish between titles and other names. Hamlet is the play; Hamlet the prince. Wuthering Heights is the novel; Wuthering Heights the house. Underlining is the equivalent in handwritten or typed manuscripts of printed italics. So what normally appears in this volume as *Othello* would be written as Othello in your essay.

Titles of articles, essays, short stories, short poems, songs, chapters of books, speeches, and newspaper articles are enclosed in quotation marks; e.g. 'The Flea' (short poem), 'The Prussian Officer' (short story), 'Middleton's Chess Strategies' (article), 'Thatcher Defects!' (newspaper headline).

Exceptions: Underlining titles or placing them within quotation marks does not apply to sacred writings (e.g. Bible, Koran, Old Testament, Gospels) or parts of a book (e.g. Preface, Introduction, Appendix).

It is generally incorrect to place quotation marks around a title of a published book which you have underlined. The exception is 'titles within titles', e.g. 'Vanity Fair': A Critical Study (title of a book about *Vanity Fair*).

Quotations

Short verse quotations of a single line or part of a line should be incorporated within quotation marks as part of the running text of your essay. Quotations of two or three lines of verse are treated in the same way, with line endings indicated by a slash(/). For example:

1 In <u>Julius Caesar</u>, Antony says of Brutus, 'This was the noblest Roman of them all'.
2 The opening of Antony's famous funeral oration, 'Friends, Romans, Countrymen, lend me your ears;/ I come to bury Caesar not to praise him', is a carefully controlled piece of rhetoric.

Longer verse quotations of more than three lines should be indented from the main body of the text and introduced in most cases with a colon. Do not enclose indented quotations within quotation marks. For example:

It is worth pausing to consider the reasons Brutus gives to justify his decision to assassinate Caesar:

> It must be by his death; and for my part,
> I know no personal cause to spurn at him,
> But for the general. He would be crowned.
> How might that change his nature, there's the question.

At first glance his rationale may appear logical . . .

Prose quotations of less than three lines should be incorporated in the text of the essay, within quotation marks. Longer prose quotations should be indented and the quotation marks omitted. For example:

1 Before his downfall, Caesar rules with an iron hand. His political opponents, the Tribunes Marullus and Flavius, are 'put to silence' for the trivial offence of 'pulling scarfs off Caesar's image'.
2 It is interesting to note the rhetorical structure of Brutus's Forum speech:

> Romans, countrymen, and lovers, hear me for my cause, and be silent that you may hear. Believe me for my honour, and have respect to mine honour that you may believe. Censure me in your wisdom, and awake your senses, that you may the better judge.

Tenses: When you are relating the events that occur within a work of fiction or describing the author's technique, it is the convention to use the present tense. Even though Orwell published *Animal Farm* in 1945, the book *describes* the animals' seizure of Manor Farm. Similarly, Macbeth always *murders* Duncan, despite the passage of time.

PART B: DOCUMENTATION

When quoting from verse of more than twenty lines, provide line references: e.g. In 'Upon Appleton House' Marvell's mower moves 'With whistling scythe and elbow strong' (l.393).

Quotations from plays should be identified by act, scene and line references: e.g. Prospero, in Shakespeare's The Tempest, refers to Caliban as 'A devil, a born devil' (IV.1.188). (i.e. Act 4. Scene 1. Line 188).

Quotations from prose works should provide a chapter reference and, where appropriate, a page reference.

Bibliographies should list full details of all sources consulted. The way in which they are presented varies, but one standard format is as follows:

1 Books and articles are listed in alphabetical order by the author's last name. Initials are placed after the surname.
2 If you are referring to a chapter or article within a larger work, you list it by reference to the author of the article or chapter, not the editor (although the editor is also named in the reference).
3 Give (in parentheses) the place and date of publication, e.g. (London, 1962). These details can be found within the book itself. Here are some examples:

> Brockbank, J.P., 'Shakespeare's Histories, English and Roman', in Ricks, C. (ed.) English Drama to 1710 (Sphere History of Literature in the English Language) (London, 1971).
>
> Gurr, A., 'Richard III and the Democratic Process', Essays in Criticism 24 (1974), pp. 39–47.
>
> Spivack, B., Shakespeare and the Allegory of Evil (New York, 1958).

Footnotes: In general, try to avoid using footnotes and build your references into the body of the essay wherever possible. When you do use them give the full bibliographic reference to a work in the first instance and then use a short title: e.g. See K. Smidt, <u>Unconformities in Shakespeare's History Plays</u> (London, 1982), pp. 43–47 becomes Smidt (pp. 43–47) thereafter. Do not use terms such as 'ibid.' or 'op. cit.' unless you are absolutely sure of their meaning.

There is a principle behind all this seeming pedantry. The reader ought to be able to find and check your references and quotations as quickly and easily as possible. Give additional information, such as canto or volume number whenever you think it will assist your reader.

SUGGESTIONS FOR FURTHER READING

Works by Chaucer

The Riverside Chaucer (Oxford, 1988), edited by Larry D Benson, is the standard volume containing Chaucer's complete works in their original Middle English form. Nevill Coghill's classic translation of *The Canterbury Tales* (Harmondsworth, 1951) is available as a Penguin paperback and remains an excellent introduction to the canon.

General introductory studies of Chaucer

Brewer, D S, *Chaucer and his World* (London, 1978)
Burrow, J A, *Mediaeval Writers and their Work* (Oxford, 1982)
Stone, B, *Chaucer: A Critical Study* (Harmondsworth, 1989)

Studies containing substantial sections on *The Pardoner's Prologue and Tale*

Cooper, H, *The structure of 'The Canterbury Tales'* (Oxford, 1983)
Kolve, V A, *Chaucer and the Imagery of Narrative: the first five 'Canterbury Tales'* (London, 1984)
Moseley, C W R D, *The Pardoner's Tale: A Critical Study* (Harmondsworth, 1987)

Longman Group UK Limited
*Longman House, Burnt Mill, Harlow, Essex, CM20 2JE, England
and Associated Companies throughout the World*

First published 1990
Second impression 1992
ISBN 0 582 06049 4

*Set in 10/12 pt Century Schoolbook, Linotron 202
Produced by Longman Singapore Publishers Pte Ltd
Printed in Singapore*

Acknowledgements
The editors would like to thank Zachary Leader for his assistance with
the style sheet.

We are grateful to Houghton Mifflin Company for permission to repro-
duce extracts from *The Riverside Chaucer*, Third Edition, edited by
Larry D Benson. Copyright © 1987 by Houghton Mifflin Company.